2010

D1259830

Scapegoats of the Empire

The True Story of Breaker Morant's Bushveldt Carbineers

Lieutenant George Witton

Front cover: Harry ("The Breaker") Morant
Back cover. The Scapegoat, by William Holman Hunt, 1854.

© Oxford City Press, 2010

INTRODUCTION

This book is dedicated to my fellow-citizens of the Commonwealth of Australia, in grateful recognition of their loyal, continuous, and successful efforts towards my release from an English prison.

I have not attempted to defend the doings of the ill-starred Bushveldt Carbineers, or the policy of those who employed them.

The methods of dealing with prisoners, which have been solely attributed to that corps, were in active operation before the so-called "Australian" officers went to the Spelonken district--a fact which the English press, and a large section of the Australian press, systematically ignored.

When I arrived in Australia, I found that the grossest misrepresentations had been made by those primarily responsible for the manner of the warfare which "staggered humanity," and that they had succeeded in linking the name of Australia with the most tragic and odious incidents connected with a mercenary and inglorious war.

If the publication of the truth will in some measure cause Australians, as a people, to take less on trust where their honour is concerned, and in future to demand the most searching enquiries and obtain definite proof before accepting the misdeeds of others as their own, then this record of an eventful experience will not have been written in vain.

GEORGE R. WITTON.
"The Elms."
Lancefield
Victoria.

Contents

CHAPTER I

VOLUNTEERING TO FIGHT "FOR THE EMPIRE"

When war was declared between the British and Boers, I, like many of my fellow-countrymen, became imbued with a warlike spirit, and when reverses had occurred among the British troops, and volunteers for the front were called for in Australia, I could not rest content until I had offered the assistance one man could give to our beloved Queen and the great nation to which I belong.

When the first Australian Contingent was being prepared for active service, I was a gunner in the Royal Australian Artillery, and was stationed at Fort Franklin, opposite Queenscliff, Victoria. I was sworn to serve for five years in the Artillery, and this gave me little hope that my wish to go to Africa would be realised. But one day a notice appeared in brigade orders that a limited number of artillerymen would be selected for service at the front, all applicants to parade on the jetty at Portsea in full marching order. Between thirty and forty attended. Soon the launch "Mars" put in an appearance from Queenscliff with Lieut.-Colonel Charles Umphelby, O.C.R.A.A., on board. (Lieut.-Colonel Umphelby was killed on active service at Driefontein in 1900.) The O.C. inspected the men, and picked out one here and there; when he came to me he looked me up and down, and remarked that I was too "big and heavy," and all my hopes were dashed to the ground. We congratulated those whom we thought were the fortunate ones, and hoped for better luck ourselves should another contingent be required.

As time went on, and reports came to hand of hard fighting and much tougher work than had been anticipated, I got more tired than ever of barrack-room soldiering, and hankered for something more real and exciting. Another call was made, another contingent was to be sent; my prospects began to brighten, but only two men were selected from the R.A.A., two quartermaster-sergeants. With the third contingent no opportunity was given to me to join. Shortly after a fourth contingent was raised, to be known as the Australian Imperial Regiment. The qualifications for the Regiment were bush experience, and that every man should be able to ride and shoot. The "machines," or the men who could merely drill and move their arms and feet as though they were worked on wire, without having the above qualifications, had no place in this contingent. I was among the successful applicants from the R.A.A., as I had been born in the bush, could ride almost as soon as I could walk, and had learned to shoot almost as soon as I learned anything. My actual military experience was gained during the twelve months I was with the R.A.A.

As soon as selected, I, with my comrades, was sent to the Victoria Barracks, Melbourne, for examination and tests. While there it was my duty to assist at the Mounted Police Depot, receiving, breaking, branding, and trucking remounts prior to sending them into camp at Langwarrin, also attending with horses at the Domain for the riding test. This riding test seemed to be looked upon by the general public as a kind of circus, and was attended daily by thousands of spectators. The track was about half a mile round, and the test was to commence at a trot, break into a gallop, and negotiate three jumps. A man could judge fairly his chance of success by the applause or "barracking" as he passed the crowd. There were many good horsemen among the recruits, men who could ride anything anywhere, and not a few who could rarely have seen a horse, much less have ridden it over a jump. One little recruit, with a very theatrical appearance, known by the sobriquet of "Bland Holt," had a great struggle to get his halter on his horse, and when it came to putting on the bridle, which was one of the Mounted Police pattern, and rather a complicated piece of harness to a new chum, he got terribly tangled up. After about ten minutes struggling, panting, perspiring, and much whoo-whoaing, he succeeded in hanging the bridle on with the bit over the horse's ears. At this stage an Artilleryman went to his rescue and saddled his horse for him. When his turn came to ride, he led his horse before the examining officer, and with much difficulty succeeded in climbing into the saddle, and started off at a walk. "Trot!" shouted the officer. The horse quickened its pace, and "Bland Holt" and his hopes of doing yeoman service for the Empire fell to the ground.

This was one of many similar incidents which took place during the fortnight the riding test lasted. About the end of March, 1900, I received orders to go into camp at Langwarrin. During the encampment there I acted as assistant to Camp Quartermaster-Sergeant Creaney, of the Hastings Battery. My duties were principally to requisition for rations and forage, and furnish returns to headquarters of any lost or worn-out equipment. On 3rd April I received my first promotion, and was made lance-corporal, and posted to the squadron under Captain J. Dallimore. This officer was very highly esteemed by all, and for bravery during the war he was promoted to the rank of major, and earned the D.S.O. While I was at Portland Prison, some years later, I learned, with the deepest regret, that the major had been accidentally drowned while fishing at Warrnambool shortly after his return to Australia.

Things went on apace in camp. The equipment department worked night and day transforming the civilian recruit into the puttied khaki soldier. Camp life was very pleasant at Langwarrin, for our friends used to come by the score, and bring well-filled hampers to picnic with us, and at night a large camp fire would be lighted and a concert held, while there was no fear of the enemy coming upon us unawares. On Sunday we were besieged by thousands of visitors, who begged earnestly from the soldiers a button or badge or some little keepsake as a memento. I myself was the recipient of several new coins, of coins with holes in them and battered halfpennies, which I was informed by the givers would bring me good luck. I am afraid I was born under an unlucky star, for if there is such a thing as luck, it did not come my way. I also received a presentation from a few of my old friends of a very nice silver-mounted letter wallet, with fountain pen and all the material necessary for a war correspondent, in order, doubtless, to keep them posted up with my experiences and doings and the number of Dutchmen I succeeded in despatching. The time passed very pleasantly, but there was another side to this--it rained in torrents for several days without ceasing, and the camp and horse lines became a veritable quagmire. It was then decided to move the camp and transfer the troops to the show-ground at Flemington. It was a memorable "trek" when we moved out for Flemington in the pouring rain; it damped the ardour of many a "contingenter," and numbers "handed in their kits." I was sent on with a fatigue party to prepare rations and forage for the rain-soaked troops and horses. But this was only for a few days; we had scarcely settled down when we were moved again to Langwarrin, and by the end of April all was in readiness for embarkation.

Lieut.-Colonel Kelly, of the Victorian Field Artillery, had been selected to command the regiment. We left Langwarrin in full marching order about midday on 28th April and reached Mentone, where we bivouacked. In the morning my horse's nosebag was missing, but I found it some months later on the South African veldt. We arrived in Melbourne about noon on 29th April, and expected to embark the same afternoon on the transport "Victorian," lying at the Port Melbourne pier. Through some hitch, the boat was not ready to receive us, and we were again quartered at the show-ground at Flemington. On Tuesday, 1st May, we broke up camp. It was a glorious and never-to-be-forgotten day, and our march through the city was signalised by an unparalleled demonstration of popular applause. The streets were packed, and in places the troops could only pass in single file. Handkerchiefs, sweets, and all kinds of good things were pressed upon us as we passed through the crowd.

On arrival at the pier, the work of embarking the horses was at once commenced, and over 700 were shipped and stalled in less than four hours. Getting the troops on board was a more difficult matter, as there was so much leave-taking and so many good-byes to say. The boat was cleared of visitors and put off from the pier, anchoring for the night opposite Williamstown. All on board was confusion and bustle, and many of the crew had been having a jolly time and were incapable of performing their duties. We got nothing that night in the shape of rations; fortunately we had our haversacks to fall back on, which provided sufficient for the day. Later on hammocks were brought out and slung. It was a new experience for me to sleep in one, and I fancy I must have slung mine too slack, for when I got into it my head and my feet almost touched, and I think I must have resembled a mammoth wood-grub in repose. We weighed anchor about 7 a.m. on Wednesday morning, and passed the heads about 11 a.m. I saw many of my old Queenscliff comrades signalling and gesticulating from the forts as we passed through the Rip. The pilot was next put off, and we were soon under way in earnest for South Africa. Cape Otway was the last

4

glimpse we had of the home land, and owing to the "Victorian" keeping well out to sea, no more land was sighted until we were off the coast of Madagascar.

As this was my first experience of a sea voyage, I fully expected that a bout of sea-sickness would be part of the programme, but such was not the case as far as I was concerned, and when I saw scores of my comrades hanging limply over the side and lying like dead men about the deck, I congratulated myself in the words of the Pharisee, "Thank God I am not as other men are." Everything on board was soon got into ship-shape order, and we lived fairly well. A large quantity of fruit and butter bad been sent on board as a gift for the use of the troops, and was greatly appreciated as a welcome addition to the bill of fare.

My duties were to assist the regimental quartermaster-sergeant, and superintend the distribution of the horse feed. This was stowed in the hold, hoisted up daily, and portioned out to the different squadrons. The horses were a splendid lot, and stood the voyage remarkably well, only one dying during the trip.

When about three days at sea a batch of stowaways made their appearance; they looked a motley and grimy crowd as they emerged from the coal bunkers. They were paraded before the ship's captain, who put them to work on the coal for the remainder of the voyage. On arrival at Beira they joined the Mashonaland Mounted Police. A little later we were paraded before the medical officers and vaccinated; it affected some very badly, and for a time they were quite incapable of doing any duty.

After about five days out I was agreeably surprised when I was informed that I had been promoted to the rank of sergeant. I was put in charge of a squad to instil into them the contents of the "Red Book" on Infantry Drill. At times, when the boat gave a roll, more turnings were gone through than were set down in the drill book.

CHAPTER II

THE VOYAGE TO AFRICA

It was now drill continuously all day and every day. Sergeant-Major Oakes, of the Victorian Rangers, held a class of instruction for non-commissioned officers every morning, and during the day Lieut.-Colonel Kelly would read to us from the bridge extracts from Queen's Regulations and Military Law, specially impressing upon us those parts which referred to the first duty of a soldier, "obedience to orders." Every Sunday church parade was held on deck; the services were conducted by the Rev. Major Holden, who accompanied us as far as Beira. Everyone had a good word for the chaplain, who was always moving about among the men, providing them with all kinds of books and writing material, and his many kindnesses were greatly appreciated by all. He edited and published a paper on board named "The A.I. Register," which was a great success. The demand for copies was so large that the supply of paper ran out, and publication ceased after the first issue.

Occasionally we would have a shooting competition between the different squadrons; an empty box or fruit case would be dropped overboard as a target, and when it was about 200 yards away we would fire volleys at it. The results were watched by a party of officers on the bridge, and points were awarded for the best shooting. Almost every evening concerts were held on deck, a very fine piano having been given for the use of the troops by the Acting-Governor of Victoria, Sir John Madden. A phonograph was also much in evidence, and at times a boxing contest would also be indulged in.

When we began to steer north-west the weather became very hot, and consequently trying for the troops, being almost unbearable day and night. Beira Harbour was reached on the morning of 22nd May, 1900. The British gunboat "Partridge" came out and met us. We were all very anxious to know how the war was going, as we had not heard any news since leaving Melbourne. Mafeking had been relieved on the 17th, but there was still plenty to do. Pretoria had not then been occupied.

We anchored in the harbour, opposite the town. The "Armenian," with the New South Wales contingent on board, had arrived a few days before, and we were greeted with ringing cheers when we dropped anchor alongside.

As there was no pier, everything had to be landed in lighters. The horses were taken off in a kind of flat-bottomed barge 20 ft. square; a tug boat would take it within a chain or so of the land, and a team of Kaffirs would then wade in and seize hold of a rope and haul it on to the beach. Owing to the harbour being full of shipping, we had rather an exciting time on one of the lighters. In dodging among the other boats, we got foul of an anchor chain, and were cast adrift, starting off with the tide at a great rate. Our tug-boat, while manoeuvring round to pick us up, was run into by another tug. After much gesticulating and vociferating on the part of the Portuguese captains, we were taken in tow again, and eventually landed on the beach.

While we were waiting in the harbour, the "Manhattan" arrived with the South Australian, West Australian, and Tasmanian contingents; she afterwards returned to Durban and landed her troops there. The 24th being the Queen's Birthday, there was a great display of bunting in the bay. At night there were fireworks, and a patriotic concert held on board. We sang "Boys of the Bulldog Breed," "Tommy Atkins," and "God Save the Queen" till "lights out."

After landing at Beira, we encamped about half a mile outside the town, adjoining the Remount Depot, where over 2000 horses, principally Hungarian ponies, were paddocked. These ponies were real little beauties to look at, and many looked fit to win a Melbourne Cup, but rather fine for remounts.

Beira is a wretched little place, built on a narrow ridge of sand along the beach. The old part of the town is built principally of galvanised iron, with here and there standing out prominently a modern building of brick, roofed with red tiles. The streets are usually ankle deep in loose sand; narrow tramways are laid down along the streets, and townspeople and tradesmen have their own private cars, which are pushed along by Kaffirs. These cars take the place of vehicular traffic, cabs and rickshaws being conspicuous by their absence. The cars are a motley collection. Some are of very rude workmanship, pushed along by a couple of dirty and almost naked Kaffirs, while others are of a more modern and aristocratic type, being hooded and upholstered, and propelled by as many as four gaily-dressed Kaffir boys. The railway (of 2-ft. gauge) and trains were built on a miniature scale; it was quite amusing to see them going along. Judging by the way the wheels went round, the smoke and noise, one would think he was travelling at least 60 miles an hour, when in reality he was travelling about six.

At this time troops were being sent into Rhodesia, and the Chartered Company was laying down a broad gauge in place of the narrow gauge between Salisbury and Beira. The contractor had completed it as far as Bamboo Creek, a malaria-stricken swamp 90 miles inland from Beira, and I wondered why the broader gauge was not pushed on to Beira, as the traffic there had become very congested. From credible information I learned that the contractors were getting #1000 per day for taking the troops through the Portuguese territory, and doubtless had their own time to do it in.

It was scandalous that thousands of men, wholly unused to such a climate, should be kept for months in such an unhealthy district, where fever and dysentery were undermining the constitutions of hundreds of them.

Several corps of Australian Bushmen had arrived at Beira just a month before us, and had gone through to Marrandellas. Some time after, the following article with reference to them was written and published in an English journal:--

To say that they were extremely annoyed would be describing their feelings too mildly.

They were very savage; they forgot themselves slightly, and swore with force and originality. They cursed Rhodesia, they cursed fate, they cursed their various Governments, but mostly they cursed their Governments, for they are a very political people these Australians, weaned on manifestoes and reared on Parliamentary debates. They cursed their Governments, knowing by heart their weaknesses, and ever ready to attribute the non-success of any undertaking--be it political, social, or warlike--to the dilatory action of certain members of the divers Cabinets.

"The Government ought never to have sent us up here at all," a Queenslander spoke with great earnestness, "if they wanted us to see any fighting. Got to Beira in April, now it's June, and--"

They were "out of it." Pretoria was occupied. This was the news which had spread the wave of pessimism over a little wayside camp on the Bulawayoroad--a camp on the fringe of the long white road, which wound south and dipped north.

The Sabakwe River trickled through the land, a stone's throw from the white tilted waggons drawn tailboard to pole to form a rough laager, and the heavy-eyed oxen stood knee-deep in its sluggish waters.

North, or rather north-east, several nights away, was Marrandellas. South of that, and far, was Beira, and it was two months ago since they had left. Two months, and Mafeking had been relieved, Johannesburg entered, Pretoria occupied. Therefore the Bushmen, who dreamt not of Eland's River, and to whom Zeerust was a name in a gazetteer, grew despondent.

"Do you think there is a chance of fighting, sir?"

I could not answer the Victorian who asked, nor did I have the heart to reprove the Tasmanian who swore.

"Well," remarked the Queenslander, "all I can say is, that if we don't see any fighting it will be a shame." He qualified shame. "We didn't come out here to be piffled through this country." There was an adjective before country. "If I wanted to admire scenery I'd have stayed in Queensland. If I wanted gold I'd have gone to Rockhampton. As for land, well, if any of you fellers want land I'll sell you a run of 6000 acres of the best land in the world."

They are peculiar, the men who are holding Eland's River; they are not soldiers as we in London know soldiers; they don't like shouldering arms by numbers, and they vote squad drill "damn silly." They are poor marching men, for they have been used to riding; they ride firmly, but not gracefully. The horses they prefer are great, rough, upstanding brutes that buck themselves into inverted V's when they are mounted, and stand on their hind legs to express their joy. The Bushman will ride a horse for a hundred miles without thinking it anything extraordinary, and bring it in in good condition, but he cannot go for a couple of miles without galloping the poor brute to death. He is very careful how he feeds his mount, and would sooner go without food himself than his dumb friend should be hungry, but it takes a troop-sergeant-major and three corporals to make a Bushman groom his horse.

They are very patient, these men; their training makes them so. They have learnt to sit by waterholes and watch sheep, dividing their time between week-old papers and day-old lambs. Politics interest them; wars--ordinary every-day war that does not call for their active interference--interest them; but the price of wool interests them more than all these things. Russian famines distress them, Indian plagues alarm them, but the blue staring sky and the rain that comes not make lines round their eyes, and puts grey into their beards.

They have got their own method of going out to fight, and that method is as distinct from that of the regular Tommy as Tommy's is foreign to the C.I.V. Tommy goes forth to battle in a workmanlike manner. He seldom writes farewell letters, but grabs a hunk of biscuit, gives his water-bottle a shake to see how much he has got, buckles on his pouches and bayonet, and, with the instinct bred on a dozen barrack squares, smooths the creases out of his stained khaki jacket. Then he picks up his rifle and eyes it critically, jerks back the bolt and squints up the barrel--Tommy, the workman, is careful of his tools--pushes back the bolt, mechanically snaps the trigger, fixes his helmet firmly on his head, and steps out to join his company.

The C.I.V. when I knew him first was somewhat self-conscious. His rifle was clean, his bandolier was ready to put on, his coat was nicely rolled, his putties were evenly fixed; long before the fall-cin bugle sounded he was ready for parade--for he was very keen. When the bugle sounded he picked up his rifle, not carelessly, as did his brother of the line, but reverently and with care. He adjusted his broad-brimmed hat, he patted his bayonet to see if it was there, and went out to face the pock-marked trenches with the proud conscious-ness that at the worst he would make a picturesque casualty.

The Bushman knows his rifle as the city man knows his walk-ing-stick. He feels neither contempt nor awe for it. It is a commercial asset, a domestic property. Perhaps he keeps his wife in dresses by shooting kangaroos; perhaps he keeps himself in whisky by tracking wallabies. His equipment is scanty. He has a bandolier, perhaps a pouch, possibly a mess-tin, certainly a "billy." When the parade-call goes he falls in with his fellows, and numbers off from the right somewhat sheepishly. On parade he is a unit and has to do as he's told, and he isn't quite used to submitting his will to those of others in au-thority.

"Fours right!"

He wheels round awkwardly. If he makes a slip he causes his horse to buck to cover his confusion.

"Walk--march!"

He is off, and he feels easier. Then comes the splitting up of his squadron into little independent patrols, and he breathes freely, for with a couple of kindred spirits on a scouting trip he is a man once more with a soul of his own. He sees most things and acts quickly. Before the "ping" of the sniper's bullet has died away he is off his horse and under cover. Then, if the sniper is an intelligent man, he won't move about much, for when a Bushman has located his quarry he can lie quite still for an hour at a stretch, his cheek touching the stock, his finger resting lightly on the trigger.

These are the men who are holding Eland's River--men who live on "damper" and tea--men whose progress through Rhodesia was marked by many dead horses and much profanity.

They wanted to fight badly. They prayed that they might get into a tight place. Their prayer is answered.

If you knew the Eland's River garrison you would not pity them, you would rejoice with them.

CHAPTER III

ROUND ABOUT BEIRA

Life in camp at Beira was almost a repetition of Langwarrin, being principally occupied in attending to and exercising the horses. On my arrival in camp I was instructed by Captain Dallimore to act as squadron-quartermaster-sergeant; my duties were to see that rations and forage were drawn daily and all camp equipment kept in order. Occasionally I went out on the veldt when exercising the horses; there appeared to be plenty of game about, and whenever a small buck rose up close to us there would be a hue-and-cry after it. Sometimes we would succeed in running it down in the long grass. It was rather dangerous sport galloping through the long grass, as one was very likely to come a nasty cropper over a hidden ant-heap. We were not allowed to take rifles out with us, but a revolver would always be forthcoming; this was used instead, but never with very great success.

On one of these outings I got my first glimpse of the Kaffirs at home. The kraals are neat little round grass huts, much resembling the old-fashioned straw bee-hives, with one small opening as a door, but so small that one would require to go on all-fours to get inside. Gaunt-looking natives, clad in only a "moucha," or loin cloth, sat lazily about, while little picaninnies, naked as when born, played around. The women, who appeared to be doing all the work, would dart inside like rabbits into a burrow when anyone approached. When we came up a group had been busily engaged round a large pot of Kaffir corn, black-looking stuff resembling linseed meal when cooked.

My opinion of the Kaffir, which was formed after later experiences, is not a good one. In his raw state, in his skins and cats' tails, he is physically and morally not a bad fellow; he will work intermittently, and much like a child, as if it were play. But as soon as he has been brought into contact with the civilising influence of the mission stations, and has discarded his cats' tails for European dress, and begins to ape the white man, he becomes a bore, and combines all the white man's vices with his own innate cunning and deceit, and his ruin is accomplished. He will not work in the hot sun, and when it is cold or raining is the most miserable of creatures, and almost incapable of work. The Dutchmen could only manage them by instilling energy into them from the end of a "sjambok."

As a fighting man the Kaffir is worse than useless. I would rather have one white man than a whole regiment of Kaffirs.

Most men who have had any lengthened experience among so-called Christianised natives, and have studied the work of the missionaries among them, are inclined to term mission stations "bosh," and the stations are rarely supported by anyone who has studied them from behind the scenes.

In return for his labour the native receives a smattering of education, and it is not unusual to meet a young native in the vicinity of a mission station with his face buried in a preparatory primer, ejaculating from memory, "I see a dog," "This is my dog," "God is my father," "God is in heaven."

As the coloured population in South Africa runs into many millions, the native question will always remain a big item in South African politics. Until polygamy and other privileges he now enjoys under tribal rights and customs are abolished the Kaffir will never become a good worker. At present he is allowed to have as many wives as he wishes; it is not "as many as he can afford to keep," for they are practically his slaves, and do the work to keep him, while he idles about the kraal smoking and drinking "joualla" or Kaffir beer. With proper legislation, management, and treatment coloured labour would never need to be imported to South Africa. The evils of the importation are seen to-day in Natal, where the Hindu holds the monopoly in many trades.

CHAPTER IV

ON THE SICK LIST

The country about Beira is very flat, and at times much of the land becomes flooded, and the roads have to be raised six or eight feet to be passable. During our stay there the Portuguese Governor and suite paid a visit to the New South Wales camp, which had been grandly decorated for the occasion with palms, banana trees, and other tropical vegetation. His Excellency greatly admired the troops and the splendid condition of the Australian horses; also Captain Ryrie's unique exhibition of boomerang throwing.

We had been at Beira nearly a month, during which time troops had been dribbling through to Rhodesia. At last it was our turn to be passed on to Bamboo Creek; we entrained at four in the after-noon, and reached Bamboo Creek at three in the morning--90 miles in eleven hours. It was considered quite a record trip. We had been very fortunate in that the train had kept on the rails the whole way without a break-down or a smash-up; I had noticed broken and overturned roll-ing-stock at intervals along the line.

About five miles out from Beira we passed through a belt of typical tropical jungle, dense undergrowth of bamboo and scrub, while overhead the trees were decked with parasite plant life, and festooned with many kinds of creeper. The Queensland bean was very promi-nent, its gigantic pods from six to eight feet in length hanging from the stems.

We stayed at Bamboo Creek four days--quite long enough, judging by the look of the cemetery opposite the camp, which had been well filled from the Imperial Yeomanry who had passed through ahead of us, a number having been employed in the workshops there building rolling-stock.

The town consisted of a couple of tin shanties, where the principal drink sold was bad wine. I had been left behind with a party of men to strike camp and gather up all camp equipment that remained, and entrain it for Umtali; I was not sorry when we got on our way. After travelling all night we stopped at Mandegas for breakfast and to feed the horses.

The country round here consists of vast plains; the landscape is bare and uninviting, and deficient in water and tree growth. After leaving Mandegas behind, the physical features of the country begin to change; isolated kopjes rise out of the veldt, and bold and picturesque outlines of ranges appear in the distance. We wound our way through the rugged gorges of Massi-Kessi, an important gold-mining district on the plateau which stretches along the Portuguese boundary, and, passing into Mashonaland, arrived at Umtali, in Rhodesia, and pitched our camp in the station yard.

I was favourably impressed with this town on account of the number and character of its buildings, its telephone service, and general up-to-date appearance; it is one of those little towns that are just moving ahead on account of the rich goldfields in the neighbourhood. It is prettily situated in a kind of great basin, almost surrounded by high mountain ranges. A little agriculture is done in this district, a settlement of Dutch farmers having been placed there by Cecil Rhodes, who himself had a model farm a little to the north.

The grass grew very long and rank, and appeared as if it would carry any number of stock. The Chartered Company afterwards put on it a thousand head of cattle which had been shipped from Australia and brought in via Beira. I afterwards met one of the men who had gone over with them and herded them at Umtali; he informed me that the experiment had been a complete failure; although they had arrived in splendid condition, the whole of them died within six months, and he had been stricken with malarial fever.

We were now in British territory, so it was decided to leave the railway and go on "trek" to Marrandellas; the Dutch settlers furnished the transports. Leaving Umtali we took the road through Christmas Pass, and rose several thousand feet as we wound our way through the mountains which encircle the town. The scenery as we rose higher and higher became more magnificent and enchanting; all around us was rank vegetation, among which ferns and beautiful wild flowers grew in great profusion, and gay-plumaged birds flitted about. Occasionally we got a glimpse of a distant landscape of fantastic and rugged grandeur, glorified by the setting sun. The climate being dry and the air so remarkably clear, even at a great distance the landscape stands out very distinctly.

We passed through Old Umtali, which had been a flourishing little settlement before the railway line was built, and had been the scene of much fighting during the last native insurrection. A mission station was about all that remained, and in its garden I noticed old rifle barrels being used to stake young fruit-trees. Along the road were deserted and tumble-down farm houses, once the homes of struggling settlers whom the natives had swooped down upon and massacred; this was made painfully evident by the lonely graves close by.

After five days' trekking through bush veldt country we reached Rusapi, a small trading station on the railway about half way between Umtali and Marrandellas; we bivouacked near the river. I shall always have a lively recollection of this camp. I turned in as usual after dark--that is, I rolled myself up in my blanket, and lay on the ground with my saddle for a pillow. It was a bitterly cold night, but being tired I soon dropped off to sleep. Towards morning I woke with a most awful pain in my right knee, which had become very stiff and much swollen. I began to think of snakes and poisonous insects, but on examination I could find no trace of anything having bitten me. With the assistance of one of my comrades I went in search of the doctor, who examined me, and informed me that I was suffering from a severe attack of "synovitis" (inflammation of the membranes of the joint). He ordered me to be taken on one of the transport waggons and to bathe my knee with cold water as often as possible.

That ride, which lasted seven days, was one of the most agonising of my experiences. I sat on the top of the waggon, which was loaded with supplies, and was unable even to lie down with any comfort, while the bumping and jolting intensified the pain until it became almost unbearable. At night, when we outspanned, I would lie under the waggon out of the night dews. Sleep was out of the question; I could only listen to the jackals and hyenas howling round the camp.

In the daytime I would try to chum in with the Dutch driver, but I found him extremely taciturn; he would sit on the front of the waggon and smoke all day, and it was only when we got stuck in a drift, or at some other tight pinch, that he would get off and flog the oxen most unmercifully. One of the oxen, which was a bit of a warrigal, or a "bi-schellum" as he termed it, he named "Englishman," and when the whip was being used poor "Englishman" received more attention than the rest of the team put together. Racial hatred was then at a very high pitch, and no opportunity was lost in giving expression to it. Although, perhaps, since peace was declared opinions are not so openly discussed, in the hearts of the Dutch race this hatred undoubtedly still exists, and is likely to exist through generations yet to come, though in the meantime it may be kept in check through the rifle and at the point of the sword.

As we continued our journey, on one occasion we got stuck in a drift or ford, among rocks and boulders. After several unsuccessful attempts to get out, our team was supplemented by another span; the result was equally unsuccessful. A third was then attached, making a span of nearly sixty oxen; again they tried to start, the drivers and natives shrieking, slashing, swearing, and shouting as though Pandemonium were let loose. This time the pole broke, and the waggon was left standing in the stream; eventually it was got upon the bank and the teams outspanned while the pole was repaired. When nearing Marrandellas the troops went on into camp, leaving the transports some five or six miles out on the road. We had camped for the night, and my leg was so stiff and painful that I could not put it to the ground. I was anxiously waiting for the morrow, when I would be able to go into hospital and get some kind of treatment.

During the evening a spring cart was sent out from the camp to the waggons for the officers' kits, and I embraced what I thought was an opportunity of getting into hospital instead of spending another night on the veldt. I was put in the cart, and all went well for about two miles, when we came to a drift with a steep bank on either side. As soon as we started on the upgrade, the horse stopped dead, and neither whip nor coaxing would make him move. After about an hour wasted in various expedients, and when the resources of the driver had been exhausted, he decided to take the brute back to camp and return with a fresh animal, promising faithfully to return in about two hours.

I lay on the ground wrapped in a horse-rug, quite alone, and waited; hour after hour passed, but no driver returned. The night was extremely cold; I had no fire, and very little covering, and I did not get a wink of sleep. All night long wild animals made the night hideous with weird and blood-curdling sounds. Lying there in the dark, help-less and unarmed, I could hear the sound of sticks breaking only a few yards away, and as my ideas of Rhodesia were largely associated with lions and other man-eating carnivora, I concluded that before morning there would be a vacancy for a sergeant in my regiment.

Shortly after daylight the driver put in an appearance, and a start was made for the camp, which was reached about 8 o'clock. After being examined by the medical officer, I was taken on to the hospital and admitted. The hospital was a low, corrugated iron building, filled with canvas stretchers, and each patient had to provide his own bed-ding, which in many cases was teeming with vermin. The food was wretched and the attendance worse.

The food consisted principally of hashed-up "Maconochie ra-tion" (a mysterious kind of tinned meat and vegetables) and boiled rice, with occasionally a bit of bread in lieu of army biscuits. This would be placed in the doorway by the cook in a couple of large pots, from which the patients had to help themselves; those who were una-ble to get up ran a risk of getting nothing at all unless they had a comrade to serve them.

There were three or four hospital orderlies, whose time ap-peared to be occupied in bossing some half a dozen Kaffir boys. I would have almost starved if I had not been able to get provisions from outside, which my comrades purchased for me from the canteen; most of this food was "commandeered" by the night orderlies while I slept. A wash was a luxury and a bath unknown. My knee had first been strapped in plaster, then blistered, and afterwards put in a splint and tightly bandaged, and I was ordered complete rest. No part of this treatment seemed to do me any good. After I had been in hospital fifteen days, a Medical Board came and sat around me, and examined me, and decided to invalid me home to Australia. I pleaded to be allowed to remain, or sent to the Cape for a change; but I was informed that it would probably be months before I would be fit for mounted duty again.

I was taken, with about forty other invalids, and put on board the train. The accommodation was disgraceful, and the management scandalous. A few men who had rheumatic fever were helpless and incapable of moving, while others were debilitated and weakened by malaria and dysentery; all were indiscriminately herded together in a couple of covered-in trucks, amongst baggage kit and rations. The rations provided consisted of the usual boulli beef and biscuits, with a little jam--no "medical comforts," not even bread.

There was one carriage on the train that was monopolised by an Imperial Yeomanry officer and a few of his men, who were being "invalided" home as useless; in his charge we were sent to the coast. Dr. Kelly, a Victorian who accompanied us, did all in his power under the circumstances. At Umtali he arranged for us to be supplied with suitable food from the railway refreshment rooms, and here we secured a stock for the remainder of the journey. Another carriage was attached to the train, and four of us commandeered a compartment, and made ourselves comfortable in a four-berth sleeper. An Imperial Yeomanry lance-corporal came along, and affecting a lot of bounce, wanted to eject us, as the room was wanted for some of his comrades. We told him what we thought of him in good Australian language, and remained in possession.

Leaving at 7 in the morning, we arrived at Beira at 11 the following day--running through without a break in the journey, as the broad gauge railway had been completed. We pulled up in the station yard, as there were then no platforms to the stations. Our kit and baggage were thrown out on the metals, and we were turned out to find our way as best we could to the Beach Hotel, where we were to be billeted. No arrangements whatever had been made to take us from the station to the hotel, a distance of about half a mile. After waiting alone for a considerable time, I hailed a good Samaritan who happened to be passing. He kindly placed his car and "boys" at my disposal, and put me down at the door of the hotel just in time for lunch, the first respectable meal I had had for months.

We remained in Beira three weeks waiting for a boat to Capetown. In the meantime, under the treatment of Dr. Kelly, my knee had greatly improved, and during the last week I was able to get about with the assistance of a stick.

It is said that when one is in Rome one must do as Rome does; the same applied to Beira. Sports, cricket matches, and bull fights are always held there on Sunday. On the second Sunday after our arrival, the opening of the Vasco Da Gama Park, which is prettily situated on a jungly sand-dune at the back of the town, took place. In the afternoon athletic sports were held. The most amusing event of the day was the natives' race, in which between three and four hundred natives of all sorts and sizes competed; native policemen were stationed round the course, and frequently used their knob-kerries upon the heads of luckless natives who tried to take a short cut.

On the Sunday following, a bull fight took place--the ideal sport of the Spanish and Portuguese nations. It had been much talked about; wild bulls had been procured, and a splendid day's sport assured. We Australians thought it rather an amusing farce. The wild bulls turned out to be a couple of hump-backed native cattle, small under-sized beasts, with very little spirit about them. One was brought in and pursued round the arena by a gorgeously-dressed matador, who annoyed and worried the poor brute by striking it with darts. When at last it turned and showed fight, it was immediately hustled out of the ring, and another of a milder disposition brought in. Much of the same by-play was gone through, but this time the matador, by a quick movement, threw a cloak over the bull's head, and falling between its horns, was carried round the arena. This final masterpiece was greeted with wild and vociferous shrieks by the onlookers.

While staying at the Beach Hotel, I made the acquaintance of Mr. Bill Upsher, a well-known South African big game hunter; he had just returned from a trip to England, and was busily engaged in fitting out a shooting expedition to the Zambesi for an Austrian count. I was extremely anxious to hear him recount a few of his experiences and

21

hair-breadth escapes, but, like many whose lives are spent chiefly in the bush, away from civilisation, and amid surroundings constantly fraught with danger, he was singularly retiring and taciturn.

In dealing with native prisoners, the Portuguese have rather a novel method, which is almost a survival of the Marshalsea of Dickens' days. Convicted natives must provide their own food, which is obtained by the sale of native work; two natives are chained together with heavy chains, and, escorted by a native policeman, are allowed to hawk their wares round the town for sale.

The Beira Constabulary, dressed in their smart khaki uniforms and Baden-Powell type of hats and armed with cutlass and revolver, are rather a formidable body of little men. In conversation with one, who could speak English well, he told me he had been a soldier and had fought in the Kaffir wars during the early settlement of the town. He became quite excited when relating his experiences, and stated that "the Kaffirs swarmed upon us in thousands, and we shot them down in millions! and then the terrible fever! and the breakdown of the commissariat! We had no food and were starving, and as a last resource had to eat dead Kaffir. The big church over the way was built in commemoration of the troops who died during that terrible war."

CHAPTER V

THE AUSTRALIANS IN CAPETOWN

On leaving Beira we embarked on the German mail-boat "Kronprinz" for Durban, calling en route at Delagoa Bay, where we remained four days discharging cargo. About 2000 tons were put off, consisting principally of tinned beef; a few lighter loads of stuff, probably munitions of war, were prohibited, and had to be put again on the boat. The number of gunboats lying in the harbour gave it the appearance of a naval station; several European nations were represented there.

This harbour is one of the finest on the east coast, the river being navigable for big shipping for nearly twenty miles. The town of Lorenzo Marques, prettily situated on rising ground on the north side, is a flourishing little place, and likely from its natural advantages to become in time the first port of commerce on the east coast. When the low-lying swamps in the neighbourhood are drained and reclaimed, malaria will no longer be dreaded, and European children will be able to grow up there with rosy cheeks.

Our pleasant voyage to Durban was marred by a tragic incident on board. One day, after the German Band had been playing as usual from the saloon deck, a bandsman who had received a slight reproof, hastened to his cabin and blew his brains out with a revolver. The incident appeared to cause but a momentary flutter; the corpse was wrapped in canvas and weighted and dropped overboard, almost before it was cold. Next day the matter was forgotten.

Durban was reached after a run of eight days. The sea was too rough to cross the bar into the harbour, and we all were well shaken as we were swung over the side in baskets on to a tender, which took us off to the landing stage.

We were now transferred to the "Persia," an ancient and rickety-looking transport, which was lying alongside the wharf. I believe she had broken her propeller shaft when taking her first load of troops to Africa; she looked as if she had been at the bottom of the sea for fifty years, and had been suddenly hauled up and set off when the war broke out. She was a splendid exhibit from the War Office, whose administrators seemed to us to consist of a number of gilt-and-tasselled drawing-room knights, sitting with their feet on velvet pile to consider the binding of a blue book or to unwind a fresh piece of red tape.

On board the "Persia" there were about 500 other invalids on their way home; the accommodation and food were in keeping with the rest of the boat. We remained at Durban for nearly a week, and were allowed to go ashore during the day; much of my time was spent in "rickshaw" rides. The "rickshaw" boys, with their grotesque headdress of feathers and horns, are fine specimens of the Zulu native; when touting for hire they fairly besiege a prospective fare, pirouetting and capering round in most striking attitudes, at the same time informing you that "Me good boy, boss!" One will go a little better with, "Me very flash boy, boss!" and start kicking up his heels and shying halfway across the road and back again. When one is selected, the others with ejaculations of disappointment return to their stands, ready to charge the next passer-by.

On Sunday a party of us drove round the Berea to Umgeni, a very pretty little pleasure resort situated among the hills, and much patronised by Durbanites; the scenery there was picturesque and pleasing, much of the country being covered with sugar plantations and orange groves. The Berea, a chain of hills at the back of the town, is the "Toorak" of Durban; splendid mansions and pretty villas peep from gardens of luxuriant tropical growth, and look out upon the town, the harbour, the Bluff, and the open sea beyond.

Leaving Durban, we arrived at Capetown after a five days' trip, which was the roughest and worst we had experienced. The "Persia" was a very narrowly-built boat, and rolled considerably, and a great sigh of relief went up from many hearts when Lion's Head and Table Mountain were sighted; we did indeed pity the poor fellows who had the ill-luck to be invalided home in such a boat.

We landed at South Arm Quay, and were drafted to the different hospitals. I was among those who went to Green Point Military Hospital, which was situated at the back of the racecourse. The racecourse was also being used as a camp for Boer prisoners of war; several thousands were quartered there.

On reception at the hospital, my kit and clothing were taken into store, and I was provided with a blue hospital suit, and was told I must not go outside the hospital grounds. The rules savoured very much of prison life, and I longed to get away from the place. The following day the medical officer came to me, and inquired my port of destination, as it was intended to ship us to Australia by the first outgoing boat. I informed him that I had no wish to return home just yet; my knee had greatly improved since leaving Rhodesia, and I would probably be fit for duty again in a few weeks. I requested to be sent to the Australasian Depot at Maitland camp. This request was granted, and two days later I was sent there. Though still very lame, I was able to get about and assist the sergeant-major with the camp duties of the depot.

Shortly afterwards the depot staff was reorganised, and I was appointed quartermaster-sergeant, an appointment which was in no way a sinecure. I had more than I could do, and with an assistant was always kept busy equipping drafts of troops for the front, attending and providing clothes to invalided men at the military hospitals at Woodstock, Wynberg, Green Point, and Rondebosch.

Maitland camp was situated about five miles from Capetown, on the left side of the Salt River, opposite the Observatory; it was the cavalry and artillery depot of the district, which included the South African Mounted Irregular Forces and all oversea colonials. The latter when off the veldt were the most difficult of any troops to deal with; when at the front they would fight and fight and face grim death without the quiver of a muscle; but it was almost a hopeless task to try to make them conform to ordinary barrack-room discipline. I had from 100 to 150 of these men under me, yet it was impossible to get more than a few on parade for camp duties.

I was often compelled, though I did it with great reluctance, to place a number of these men under arrest for insubordination; the effect it had on them was not worth the trouble. The only time I could rely on getting a full muster was at "pay parade," which was most religiously attended. On one occasion the camp regimental sergeant-major required a number of men and instructed me to parade every available man at once. I immediately went to the Australians' quarters and shouted, "Fall in for pay!" This had the desired effect. I secured about fifty, and handed them over to the regimental sergeant-major, to the surprise and disappointment of many sick, lame, and tired "soldiers of the King" who had been disturbed from their afternoon's naps. Vengeance upon me was mooted, and "tossing in a blanket" suggested. They had been grievously taken in; their annoyance passed off, however, and in a few days I had the intense satisfaction of taking them to the docks and embarking them for home. Old scores were then forgotten, and as the tender put off they gave three cheers for their sergeant-major, an honour which greatly amused me and was as much appreciated.

These men were not altogether to blame; they should never have been sent to Maitland, which was a duty camp. They had been crowded out of the hospitals as soon as convalescent, and sent there to await embarkation, instead of being sent to a convalescent depot. They absolutely refused to mount guard or do picquet and fatigue duties. During this time the bubonic plague was raging in Capetown, and a plague camp was established near Maitland. One day the New South Wales Mounted Rifles arrived in camp from up-country, and while waiting to embark for home were ordered to furnish guards for the plague camp. A non-commissioned officer refused to do this duty, and was court-martialled and sentenced to three months' imprisonment, which he underwent at the Castle Military Prison, Capetown.

This punishment was, I suppose, merited for insubordination; but these men had been fighting nobly and well at the front, and on the eve of their departure for home should not have been called upon to do duty at an infectious disease camp. The day following they would probably be rushed on to a crowded transport, and scandals similar to that of the "Drayton Grange," where men died like rotten sheep from an infectious disease, were inevitable; even a dreaded plague might be scattered broadcast wherever they might land.

During the plague scare at Capetown a case occurred in the men's quarters at the Australasian depot. It happened at a most inopportune time, and the results were disastrous. Preparation had been made to despatch a batch of invalids home; everything was in readiness, the men had their kits packed, and were being put through a medical examination prior to leaving camp, when one man, a New South Wales Artilleryman, was found to have symptoms of plague. This necessitated the whole of the men being quarantined and removed from their quarters. A camp under canvas was formed near the bank of the Salt River; the men were extremely annoyed, and vented their spite on the offending huts. They armed themselves with sticks, stones, and a couple of axes, and raided their late quarters. They smashed every window, broke down the doors, tables, and forms, and hacked and hewed at the iron walls. In a few minutes the place was almost demolished, and it was intended to finish up by setting fire to the ruins, but progress was stopped by the arrest of four of the ringleaders. These were called upon for the amount of the damages, which was paid without a murmur. The men afterwards wrecked a newspaper office in Capetown, the journal published there having passed disparaging remarks on their previous actions at Maitland, and on Australians generally.

The Canadians were attached to the Australasian depot. These men were some of the finest irregular soldiers that ever carried a rifle. There were miners from Klondyke, hunters from the backwoods, troopers from the Northwest Frontier Police, and included were some of the "hardest cases" that the land of the maple leaf ever produced; these were past-masters in the use of unique expletives, and for downright and original profanity it would hardly be possible to find their equal. An officer would remonstrate with his men in most candid terms, but for all this they were the men above all others for a tight place or a desperate enterprise, and they rigidly adhered to the rule of never allowing their enemies to trouble them a second time.

SCAPEGOATS OF THE EMPIRE

The following poem appeared about this time in "The Navy Illustrated":--

Oh, bitter blew the western wind and chilled us to the bone, From mountain top to mountain top it made its weary moan, While we, Strathcona's Horse, rode on, in silence and alone.

The darkness closed around us like a monk's hood gathered tight, It pressed upon our eyeballs, sealing up the sense of sight, And mocked us with false flashes of a brain-begotten light.

With straining at the silence grew our hearing thunder-proof; The moaning blast in vain flung back its echo from the kloof, The very ground on which we rode struck dumbly to the hoof.

And no man spake, nor dared so much as loose his tethered tongue, Which else in fevered agony from blackened lips had hung, But now, with limpet grip compelled, to cheek and palate clung.

Strathcona's Horse had never borne the fear mark on their brow; The oak sap was their blood--the thews, the supple maple bough; Their swords were fashioned from the share that shod their prairie plough.

Then why those white, drawn faces? Why those breasts that strain and heave? Those eyes that see but darkness? And those tongues that parch and cleave? It was the tale the Zulu scout brought southward yester eve.

It was the same old tale--the farm, the false white flag, the foe; And four good British lads that fell where murder laid them low. Strathcona's Horse their purpose knew--the morning, too, should know.

On! on! there's twenty miles and more between us and the prey, And still the scout, with bleeding feet, directs our weary way, And still our eyes strain eastward for the coming of the day.

A dark ravine, whose beetling sides o'erhang the path we tread-- A faint grey line, a spot of light, with shimmering haze o'er-

28

spread-- A wreath of smoke--the farm, the farm, six hundred yards ahead.

But see--the Zulu lied. God bless that faithless, perjured black! Those British lads died not, but live. On yonder chimney stack Behold, wrapped in the morning mist, our flag, the Union Jack!

Strathcona's Horse rode forward with a swift Canadian swing, Their hearts with joy o'erflowing, and the teardrops glistening--Ping! Halt! What was that? Hell's fury! 'twas the Mauser's deadly ring.

Oh, fathomless the treacherous depths within the Boer breast! It was the foe had raised that flag above their devil's nest, While stark and stiff four corpses lay where murder bade them rest.

Strathcona's Horse rode forward, though there fell both horse and man; They spake no word, but every brain conceived the self-same plan: Through every vein and nerve and thew the self-same purpose ran.

What though the Mausers raked the line, and tore great gaps between? What though the thick clay walls stood firm, the ambushed foe to screen? There was a deed to do, whose like the world had seldom seen.

They stormed the palisades, which crashed beneath their furious stroke; The doors with staves they battered in, the barricades they broke-- And then they bound the fiends within, with Mausers for a yoke.

Swift to the ending of the deed, yet only half begun, The daylight grows: there's bloody work still waiting to be done-- Six corpses swing athwart the face of God's own rising sun.

Bury in peace our own dear dead;--then comrades, ride away; Yet leave a mark that all may know, who hitherward shall stray, Strathcona's Horse it was that paid a visit here to-day.

'Twas thus Strathcona's Horse left Vengeance sitting by her shrine, Where six accursed corpses broke the grey horizon line, Their flesh to feed the vultures, and their bones to be a sign.

I also extract the following from a South African paper published in April, 1901:--"A member of Strathcona's Horse writes to me of the gratification felt by that body at having been the first regiment to be presented with the King's colours in recognition of services rendered on the field of battle. It is described as a Union Jack of silk, trimmed with gold, and having gold tassels, and at the top of the staff a gold crown surmounted by a lion. To the flagstaff is fixed a silver plate, engraved with a crown and this inscription:--'Presented by His Majesty the King to Lord Strathcona's Corps, in recognition of services rendered to the Empire in South Africa--1900.'"

On one occasion, when embarking invalids for Australia on board the "Persic," which was lying in the roadstead in Table Bay, I met several old acquaintances. I had been in conversation with them down below for about ten minutes, when to my great consternation I felt the vibration of the engines, and found that the "Persic" was on her way to Australia. I rushed to the bridge and called the captain, and informed him of my predicament; he stopped the boat, which by this time had passed outside the breakwater, and hailing a sailing smack that happened to be passing, I, with no little difficulty, got on board and was landed at the docks again. A man never knows his fate; what seemed to me then to be a stroke of ill-luck may have been a visit from my guardian angel in disguise, for, as subsequent events proved, it would perhaps have been better for me if the "Persic" had carried me away unawares to Australia.

After being about four months at Maitland camp, I as anxious to rejoin my regiment. My knee, to all appearance, was perfectly well, and I had got rid of my lameness, though during this time I had not attempted to ride a horse. Then Lord Roberts was about to come to Capetown to embark for home, and I was selected to form one of the escort to meet him on his arrival. As soon as I began to take mounted exercise my knee again became troublesome, and my eagerness to take part in the reception cost me another three months' limping.

THE AUSTRALIANS IN CAPETOWN

Some time after this the camps at Maitland were closed, and the Cavalry, Artillery, Irregular and Imperial Yeomanry troops were concentrated at the Military Camp on the Green Point Common. The common was once a beautiful grassy down, but the traffic of a large camp had so ploughed it up that it was knee deep in loose sand, and the wind, almost constantly blowing, carried sand with it everywhere.

CHAPTER VI

COMMISSIONED IN THE BUSHVELDT CARBINEERS

About this time I made the acquaintance of Major Lenehan, officer commanding the Bushveldt Carbineers, and had a conversation with him regarding a commission in his corps. He told me that he was about to get a gun section attached to it, and if I could raise a detachment of men he would give me command. I recruited a number of time-expired Australians, and several Imperial Royal Horse Artillerymen. On several occasions I applied for my discharge to enable me to take up my commission, but this was not permitted until my regiment returned home for disbandment.

In June, 1901, I embarked on the "Orient" at Capetown and rejoined my regiment at East London. There I received a temporary discharge from the Victorian Imperial Bushmen. I received a telegraph message from the O.C.B.V.C., Pietersburg, informing me that my appointment as lieutenant had been confirmed, and directing me to proceed to Pietersburg with any men I could get together there. I prevailed upon thirty returning Australians to remain and join the Carbineers and form the gun detachment. I had them sworn in and equipped at the local recruiting depot.

The saddlery issued to these men was practically useless. How any man or body of men could pass such worthless shoddy is beyond comprehension, and reflects sadly on the judgment of the Supplies

Board. The saddles were without a vestige of stuffing, and the stirrup-irons were cumbersome pieces of ironwork, weighing over 7 lbs., and so narrow that an ordinary-sized boot would not fit into them--just the kind of equipment to cripple the rider and ruin the horse at the same time. As soon as it was taken into camp at Pietersburg the whole of it was condemned and returned to the ordnance stores.

While at East London with a few others, I went one day into a cafi for lunch. We met a young fellow there who had come from Gippsland, Victoria. He had been drinking rather heavily during his stay in the town. He sat down at the table, and was served with soup; when he had finished he got up to pay for it and go out. He was not hungry, and did not care for anything to eat; he only felt thirsty. "How much for the soup?" he inquired. "Half a crown for the dinner," was the reply. "But I only had a plate of soup!" "That makes no difference; you pay for the dinner." So he sat down again and called for more soup. Another and another was called for, until six plates had been served; then he paid for the dinner, and went out satisfied that he had had his money's worth, and had not been "taken down."

On 4th July I left East London en route for Pietersburg. During the day United States citizens were to be seen in gay attire driving through the town, displaying little flags of the Stars and Stripes. They were celebrating their national holiday.

Leaving by the evening mail train with the troops I had recruited, we reached Queenstown the following morning. Branching off at Stormberg Junction, we went on to Nauupoort, where the train stabled for the night. The following day we reached Norval's Pont; we travelled then only in the daytime, and reached Pretoria on the afternoon of the 11th.

As there was no train to Pietersburg until the following day, I spent a little time looking round Pretoria, visiting the church square, which is surrounded by the Government buildings of the late Republic, and in the centre of which stood the unfinished statue of President Kruger, a striking parallel to the nation of which he had been the head. I then visited Kruger's church and residence, with its two white lions guarding the entrance with silent irony.

Close to the railway station is the public market square, which in days before the war would be crowded with the waggons and teams of the Boer farmers, who came to sell or barter their odds and ends of farm produce. Near by was the Pretoria Museum, containing much-prized relics of their old voortrekkers, of their earlier wars and Jameson's raid, and specimens of South African game. This was a great resort of the Boer farmer to instruct the rising generation in the history of their country. After admiring the old guns with which they had fought so bravely and so well, they would turn to a model of one of Donald Currie's liners--"There is the big ship that brings the rooineks over the sea water." Then, pointing to an assvogel--"There is the bird that eats the rooineks when we shoot them like bushbuck on the veldt."

Leaving Pretoria on the morning of the 12th July, we passed Haman's Kraal, where the previous night there had been some sharp fighting, and the Dutchmen had got away with a number of cattle; the armoured train picked us up here and escorted us to Nylstroom, where we remained for the night. Kitchener's Fighting Scouts were lying alongside the station, having come in to refit. In the morning I met Major Lenehan, who had arrived by train from Pietersburg. I paraded my men for inspection, and was complimented for my efforts in getting together such a fine troop of men.

Leaving Nylstroom for Pietersburg, we passed a spot at Naboonspruit which was marked by nineteen fresh graves. Only a few days before a train had been wrecked there by Boers; an officer, Lieutenant Best, of the Gordon Highlanders, a personal friend of the late Captain Hunt and Lieutenant Morant, had been killed, also eighteen men, including the driver, firemen, and guard of the train. I saw the truck at Warm Baths Station in which these men were shot down; the iron walls had been about as much protection from Mauser bullets as a sheet of paper; the truck was riddled like a sieve. On arrival at Pietersburg, I was met by Lieutenants Edwards and Baudinet; the latter I had known for some time at Capetown, and a few months previously I had acted as best man at his wedding.

CHAPTER VII

THE ORIGIN OF THE CARBINEERS

Pietersburg is an important town 180 miles north of Pretoria and the terminus of the railway. After the occupation of Pretoria in June, 1900, the Boer Government was set up here, and it was not until May, 1901, that the town was occupied and garrisoned by British troops.

A tragic incident, in which two Tasmanian officers were killed, is related to have occurred on the day the troops entered Pietersburg. These two officers were going out to a magazine on the outskirts of the town, and were sniped at and shot dead by a Dutch schoolmaster who lay hidden in the long grass. When the troops ran up to see what was the matter, this gentleman jumped up, and, holding up his hands, shouted, "I surrender! I surrender! I surrender!" The men walked up to him, and without hesitation ran a bayonet through his body, and in the heat and stress of the battlefield this action of the soldiers was applauded.

My duties as an officer of the Carbineers began on 13th July. There was little to be done, and less to be learned, in the ordinary routine of camp duty, which consisted principally of attending the stables to see that the men fed and groomed their horses.

When I had been about a fortnight at Pietersburg Major Lenehan returned from Pretoria; he had not succeeded in getting guns for his gun section, and ordered me, much against my inclination, to take over the quartermaster's duties from Lieutenant Mortimer. I held this position about a week.

The Bushveldt Carbineers were raised in Capetown and Pretoria early in 1901 for special service in the Northern Transvaal. A Mr. Levy, a storekeeper at Pienaar's River, who had made some money out of the Pienaar's River garrison, offered to devote part of his savings towards the formation of a mounted corps to operate in that district. He contributed #500; Mr. M. Kelly, merchant, of Pietersburg, also gave #100; Dr. Neel, of Matapan, Spelonken, #100; a few others also subscribed. It was orginally proposed to raise 500 men, but not more than 350 constituted the full strength.

The camp and headquarters of the Carbineers formed part of the Pietersburg garrison, which was made up of the 2nd Wiltshire Regiment, 2nd Gordon Highlanders, a section of the Royal Field Artillery, and a detachment of the Royal Garrison Artillery, with a 5-in. gun, which was known throughout the war as a "cow-gun," on account of it being drawn by oxen. Colonel Hall, C.B., was garrison commandant. The other officers of the corps stationed at Pietersburg while I was there were Major Lenehan, Lieutenant and Adjutant Edwards, Lieutenant and Quartermaster Mortimer, Lieutenant Baudinet, all Australians, and all late members of the first Australian contingents. There were also Lieutenant Neel, an English doctor, and Lieutenant Kelly, a Pietersburg merchant.

A detachment of the Carbineers was at Strydspoort, a post about 35 miles south-east of Pietersburg, and was under the command of Lieutenant H. H. Morant. Another detachment was at Fort Edward, Spelonken, 90 miles north from Pietersburg. This detachment was sent there to assist Captain Alfred Taylor, a special service officer, and was under the command of a captain of the Carbineers; with him went Lieutenant Handcock, a veterinary officer.

Major Lenehan was officer commanding the Carbineers, but in reality this was in rank and name only. The major rarely visited the outposts, which were practically under the direct control of the officers in charge; he was a good-natured man, and much attached to his officers.

THE ORIGIN OF THE CARBINEERS

There has been argument regarding the nationality of Lieutenant Morant, and the ignominy of his fate has in prejudiced quarters been attached to Australia. He was, however, born in England and reared as an English gentleman, coming to Australia in manhood. There he was engaged in various bush avocations, especially in droving and breaking horses; hence the pen-name of "The Breaker," by which he became known as a popular writer of verses. He went to the war with an Australian contingent; a good fellow, one could not help liking him, yet he was very hot-headed, and usually did things on the impulse of the moment. He exacted strict obedience, and obtained it, where others holding a much higher rank might have failed.

Captain Taylor was a special officer of the Intelligence Department, and worked the wild and isolated part of the Transvaal around Spelonken. He was an Irishman by birth, but had lived a number of years in Africa among the natives; he had been a lieutenant in Plumer's Scouts in the Matabele War, and had command of a corps of Cape boys. He had been selected and sent to the Spelonken by Lord Kitchener, on account of his knowledge of the natives. As far as the natives were concerned, he had a free hand and the power of life and death; he was known and feared by them from the Zambesi to the Spelonken, and was called by them "Bulala," which means to kill, to slay. He had the power to order out a patrol when he required it, and it was generally understood that he was the officer commanding at Spelonken. At the trials of the officers later on he admitted in evidence that he had held this position.

CHAPTER VIII

WHAT LED TO THE TROUBLE

The officer who had command of the detachment of Carbineers assisting Captain Taylor was, as it appeared, altogether unfit to command such a body of men, and allowed his detachment to drift into a state of insubordination verging on mutiny. The men did almost as they liked, and horses and other captured stock were being divided amongst themselves, while stills on neighbouring farms were freely made use of. According to the evidence taken at the court martial (which is extracted from a summary that appeared in the "Times," 18th April, 1902), Captain Taylor on 2nd July, 1901, received intelligence that a party of six armed Boers were going into the camp to surrender. The officers in charge decided to intercept these men, and not allow them to come in; they would send out a patrol and have them ambushed and shot. After a good deal of argument, a sergeant-major paraded a patrol, headed by a sergeant. The men were told to go out and meet the waggon in which were the six Boers; they were to make the Boers fight, and on no account were these to be brought in alive; if the white flag was put up the men were to take no notice of it, just fire away until all the Boers were shot. This, I afterwards learned, was the correct interpretation of the orders not to take prisoners.

The patrol went out, met the six Boers, and opened fire on them. The Boers at once put up the white flag and made a great noise; so, thinking there might be women and children in the waggon, the patrol ceased firing and went to look, but as there were only six men, they were taken out and shot. It has been stated that these men had a large sum of money in their possession, but the money was all a myth. I never heard of any money being taken from them. The Boers invariably buried their money for safety, and I have no doubt large sums of money still remain buried in different parts of the Transvaal.

The next incident of note which occurred was the shooting of a trooper of the Fort Edward detachment, and it is here that Lieutenant Handcock first appears in connection with the troubles of the Carbineers. Handcock was an Australian, and was never the bloodthirsty desperado that (after he had been shot) he was made out to be; he was simply the chosen tool of unprincipled men, who held the power to command. He was born and reared to bush pursuits, and was a hard worker; if he was not doctoring the back of a worn-out horse, he was at the forge shoeing. He never initiated any outrage, but he had a keen sense of duty, and could be absolutely relied upon to fulfil it. He had been seen under fire many times, and there never was a braver man. The trooper who had been shot was a Boer, and he had been allowed to become a member of the Carbineers, but there were strong suspicions that he was acting the traitor. There were a number of prisoners in the camp, and this trooper frequently absented himself, while on one occasion he was seen and heard pointing out among his comrades the men who had despatched his six unfortunate countrymen.

No officer was ever brought to trial for having this man shot, but Major Lenehan was charged with having failed to report his death, and for this he was reprimanded. A report had been sent in, which had been "edited" by the three officers immediately concerned, and it was made to appear that this trooper had been shot in a brush with the Boers. This was stated at the court-martial to have been done in the interest of the corps. About this time the officer in charge of the detachment requested to be recommended for the Distinguished Service Order in recognition of his services.

Later on an allegation was made by a lady against an officer in the Spelonken district, and, upon inquiries being made by the authorities at Pietersburg, he was recalled, and was given the option of standing his trial at a court-martial or resigning his commission. He sent in his resignation, and left the corps.

Captain Taylor was afterwards tried by court-martial for having ordered the shooting of the six Boers. Captain Robertson elected to turn King's evidence. Taylor was promptly acquitted, as he was also on the charge of shooting a native. A late brother officer informed me that after Morant and Handcock had been shot, and I had become "the guest of the nation" for an indefinite period, Captain Taylor was promoted to another important position in the Transvaal.

CHAPTER IX

DEATH OF CAPTAIN HUNT--MORANT'S REPRISALS

When Captain Robertson was recalled from Fort Edward, Captain Hunt, who was on special duty in Pretoria, and had formerly held a commission in the 10th Hussars, was sent to supersede him. Captain Hunt was accompanied by Lieutenants Morant and Hannam, an Australian; Lieutenant Picton, an Englishman, afterwards joined them. I was not personally acquainted with Captain Hunt, but evidently he had been held in high esteem by officers and men alike, and he was always referred to by them as a fine fellow and a thorough "white man."

Lieutenant Picton took with him a convoy, with regimental stores, among which was a quantity of rum for the use of the troops; on the way out some of the men looted this, and what they did not drink they hid away. After their arrival at Fort Edward they would periodically leave, and return to the fort in a state of intoxication. This led to Captain Hunt placing several of them under arrest for insubordination, and also for threatening to shoot Lieutenant Picton. At night these men broke their arrest and rode into Pietersburg. Captain Hunt sent in a report, and made charges of a serious nature against them to Major Lenehan, who caused them to be again placed under arrest, pending court-martial proceedings. Upon a preliminary inquiry being made as to their conduct, they made disclosures regarding what was going on at Spelonken. When the matter was brought before Colonel

Hall, C.B., garrison commandant, it was decided in the interests of all concerned to discharge them from the regiment and let them go. To these men may be credited the monstrous and extravagant statements and lying reports about the Carbineers which appeared later in the English and colonial press.

After the preliminary courts of inquiry held some time after this into the charges against officers of the Carbineers, and before the courts-martial were held, Colonel Hall was suddenly recalled by the War Office, relieved of his command, and sent out of the country to India.

Captain Hunt found affairs in a very disorganised state at Fort Edward, and immediately set about to rectify them. He had the stock collected and handed over to the proper authorities, and the stills broken up. These reforms were carried out by Lieutenants Morant and Handcock, and this was one of the reasons why these two officers were disliked (or "detested," as a returned Carbineer put it) by certain members of the detachment.

It was decided at this time to send twenty additional men out to Captain Hunt, with Lieutenant Baudinet in command, but owing to an accident which that officer had met with while playing polo, he was unable to go, and I was selected in his place.

I left Pietersburg on 3rd August with Sergeant-Major Hammett and twenty men, and arrived at Fort Edward the following evening. Lieutenant Hannam met me some distance out from the fort, and accompanied me in. He introduced me to Lieutenants Morant and Handcock. This was the first time I had met these officers.

Lieutenant Picton was away at Chinde with a patrol, and Captain Hunt was away with another party in the Majajes district. He was killed on the night of 5th August, 1901, when making an attack upon Commandant Viljoen's farmhouse at Duival's Kloof, a spot about 80 miles east of Fort Edward. Captain Hunt had with him only a small party of his own men, seventeen in number, as he had been informed by natives that there were only twenty Boers in occupation of the farmhouse; he had with him also a number of armed natives.

It was stated at times during the war by those in authority that the natives were not permitted to take any part in the fighting, but such was not the case. During the time I was in the Spelonken district with the Carbineers the natives were twice raised, and it has been openly stated that, with the connivance of others, when Colonel Grenfell went through the district, he had thousands of these savages, who were fed and paid, attached to his column, and they committed the most hideous atrocities, which no one has yet been made to account for.

The natives would follow a patrol like a flock of vultures, armed with all kinds of weapons, from a cowhide shield and bundle of assegais to the latest pattern of rifle. They were worse than useless in action. They might fire one shot, but would then clear out and hide in the long grass until the fighting was over, appearing again on the scene to loot and plunder everything they could lay their hands on.

It was the intention of Captain Hunt to rush the farmhouse at night, and surprise the Boers, but the Boers surprised the patrol, and instead of only twenty, there were fully eighty in possession. On making the attack, they were met by a withering fire. At the first volley the natives turned and fled, and I was told by an eye witness that some of the uniforms of Hunt's attacking party could be seen beating a hasty retreat with them.

Captain Hunt and two sergeants reached the house, and commenced firing through the windows. They shot down several of the Boers, Commandant Viljoen being amongst them. Captain Hunt was himself then shot in the breast, and fell off the verandah to the ground, where he lay moaning. He was seen by one of his sergeants, who could not render him any assistance on account of the continuous firing from the house and from their own men behind. Sergeant Eland was also shot dead; he was the son of a local settler, whose farm adjoined Reuter's Mission Station. He had formerly been a member of the Natal Carbineers, and had seen much service on the Natal side at the outbreak of the war. He subsequently joined the Bushveldt Carbineers, and was killed within a few miles of his own home, where he was taken and buried.

Towards morning the Carbineers withdrew to Reuter's Mission Station, about five miles away, and from there despatched a message to Fort Edward, reporting the loss of Captain Hunt and Sergeant Eland, and asking to be reinforced without delay.

Early on Wednesday morning the news reached Fort Edward, and its effect upon Morant was terrible; instead of being the usual gay, light-hearted comrade whom I had known for three days, he became like a man demented. He ordered out every available man to patrol before Captain Taylor at his office at Sweetwaters Farm, about one mile from the fort.

Morant tried to address the troops, but broke down, and Captain Taylor then spoke a few words to them, urging them to avenge the death of their captain, and "give no quarter." Guides and intelligence agents were furnished by Taylor, and the patrol started off with Morant in command. We travelled across country, and took the most direct route to Reuter's Station. When we were about twenty miles out, we met Lieutenant Picton returning, with a number of prisoners, who were, by the order of Lieutenant Morant, handed over to a small escort, and sent on to Fort Edward. Picton and the remainder of his men were attached to the patrol. This was my first meeting with Lieutenant Picton.

We hurried on, and made a forced march, off-saddling every four hours or so to give the horses a rest, and then on again. At times the guide, who was a German, would lose his way, and a halt would be called. Morant, who was in no mood to be trifled with, and thought he was doing it on purpose, would rage and curse and upbraid and threaten him, until he became afraid of his life.

By nightfall we had covered more than 40 miles, and then put up at a native kraal to give the horses a feed and wait until the moon rose. Here one of the intelligence agents left us to gather up an army of natives. By the faint light of a new moon, we started at one o'clock in the morning, and had much difficulty in finding our way, our guide continually misleading us. Once, in crossing a swampy stream, he missed the ford, and horses and men were floundering about in a deep muddy bog, several of the latter getting a dirty morning dip.

By midday we reached the Letaba Valley, in the Majajes Mountains, inhabited by a powerful tribe of natives once ruled by a princess said to be the prototype of Rider Haggard's "She." One huge, brawny native recalled to me Allan Quartermain's doughty old warrior Umslopogaas.

Passing along the valley, through some of the most rugged landscape secnery in South Africa, we reached Reuter's Mission Station about four in the afternoon. Here we met the men of Captain Hunt's patrol; they had just one hour before buried their captain. After visiting his grave, we returned to Mr. Reuter's house, where Lieutenant Morant interrogated several men regarding Captain Hunt's death. They were all positive that he had met with foul play; they were sure his neck had been broken, as his head was rolling limply about in the cart when he was being brought in. His face had been stamped upon with hob-nailed boots, and his legs had been slashed with a knife; the body was stripped completely of clothes and lying in a gutter when found. Mr. Reuter and Captain Hunt's native servant, Aaron, who had washed and laid out his body for burial, corroborated these statements.

This convinced Morant that his brother officer and best friend had been brutally murdered; he vowed there and then that he would give no quarter and take no prisoners. He had ignored his orders to this effect in the past, but he would carry them out in the future. I was informed that Captain Hunt had paraded his officers and sergeants, and told them that he had direct orders from headquarters at Pretoria not to take prisoners. Morant repeated these orders to me as they were given to him by Captain Hunt.

We remained at the Mission Station waiting for runners to come in from the intelligence agents, who had been watching the movements of the Boers. At daybreak in the morning, news came that they had vacated the farmhouse at Duival's Kloof, and were trekking away towards the Waterberg. They had a clear day's start of us, but we went off with about forty-five men, leaving a few behind to guard the Mission Station, which the Boers had threatened to bum down over Mr. Reuter's head because our troops had been harboured there.

Morant rode at the head, gloomy and sullen, and eager to overtake the retreating enemy. I was in command of the rearguard. We rode hard all day, only resting once to give the horses a handful of mealies we had brought with us. Just at sunset the advance guard sighted the Boers, who had laagered for the night in a hollow at the foot of a chain of kopjes. Morant was excited and eager to make an attack. He sent Lieutenant Picton with a party of men on the right flank, but to Morant, in his excitement, the moments seemed hours. Before Picton could get his men into position, and just as I arrived at the foot of the kopje with the rearguard, Morant opened fire on the laager. I dismounted my men and hastened to the top. Looking down, I could see the camp fires and hear the Boers crying out, "Allamachta! Allamachta" ("God Almighty!"), and shouting to each other in great consternation. Ceasing fire, we moved on rapidly, and rushed the laager, only to find that the Boers had jumped on their horses and ridden away, leaving behind their waggons, blankets, and everything they possessed. Several dead and wounded horses were lying about, and underneath a waggon we found a Boer wounded in the heel. Lieutenant Morant insisted that he should be shot on the spot, but he was prevailed upon not to do this, as the firing might attract the Boers, who nearly doubled us in number, and it was necessary to withdraw to a safe position for the night. A Cape cart with mules inspanned was found in the laager; the prisoner, Visser by name, was put in it, and all drew back to a neighbouring kopje, where we bivouacked.

Although tired out, there was no possibility of any sleep, as it was necessary to keep on the qui-vive in case the Beers should pay us a surprise visit. Outposts had to be visited to see that the men were on the alert. The night was intensely, cold, and we had had nothing to eat since leaving the mission station. We had travelled with stripped saddles to make it as light as possible for the horses. On this march I found strong coffee very sustaining, and I have often travelled all day on an occasional cup of this beverage.

Early the following morning a native runner brought a message to Morant from Fort Edward requesting him to return with all speed. The fort, with only a few men in charge, was in danger of being attacked by a party of Boers who were in the neighbourhood. Our horses were about knocked up, so Morant decided to give up the pursuit of the Boers and return to the fort. Before setting out, he examined and questioned Visser, and found in his possession articles of clothing, a tunic called a "British Warm," and a pair of trousers which he identified as the property of the late Captain Hunt. He informed me and others that the first time we outspanned he would have Visser shot.

After burning the waggons and collecting the oxen, we started on our homeward journey, I, as before, following with the rearguard.

About 11 o'clock the patrol halted near Mameheila, on the Koodoo River. A beast was slaughtered here, and I broke my fast on a very tough piece of trek-ox steak. During the morning Lieutenants Morant and Handcock had discussed Visser's position, and had decided to shoot him as soon as we halted. Upon my arrival with the rearguard, Morant came to me and again informed me that it was his intention to have Visser shot. "This man," he said, "has been concerned in the murder of Captain Hunt; he has been captured wearing British uniform, and I have got orders direct from headquarters not to take prisoners, while only the other day Lord Kitchener sent out a proclamation to the effect that all Beers captured wearing khaki were to be summarily shot." I asked him to leave me out of it altogether, as I did not know anything about the orders, I had been such a short time there. Morant then walked away, and ordered Sergeant-Major Clarke to fall-in ten men for a firing party. Some of the men objected, and the sergeant-major came and asked me if I would speak to Morant on behalf of those men.

I went to Morant as requested, but found him obdurate. "You didn't know Captain Hunt," he said, "and he was my best friend; if the men make any fuss, I will shoot the prisoner myself." After a little delay, men volunteered--"to get a bit of our own back," one remarked. Lieutenant Picton was placed in command of the firing party, and Visser was shot.

I did not witness the execution or take any part whatever in it. To the best of my knowledge this was the first prisoner shot by the order of Lieutenant Morant, and the motive for the execution was purely that of retaliation for an outrage committed upon a British officer.

War is calculated to make men's natures both callous and vengeful, and when civilised rules and customs are departed from on one side, reprisals are sure to follow on the other, and the shocking side of warfare in the shape of guerilla tactics is then seen. At such a time it is not fair to judge the participants by the hard and fast rules of citizen life or the strict moral codes of peace. It is necessary to imagine one's self amidst the same surroundings--in an isolated place, with the passions of war aroused, men half-starved, dangers constantly threatening from all quarters, and responsibilities crowding one upon another--to enable a fair decision to be reached.

The intelligence agent, who had left us to raise the natives, now returned with several hundred savages, but as their services were not now required, they were fed, and, when they had held a war dance, were dispersed. Continuing our homeward journey, we arrived at Hay's store, 18 miles from Fort Edward, about midnight, and rested there until daylight.

Mr. Hays was a British trader, and with his wife and family kept a store in a wild part of the Spelonken. He was well-known for his hospitality to our troops. After our departure a party of marauding Boers, who knew of this, swooped down upon him, and looted him of everything he possessed, even dragging the wedding ring from his wife's finger.

There were numerous bands of these marauders in the district roving about, commandeering all they could lay their hands upon, wrecking trains, or doing any bushranging job that presented itself to them. When they were nearly starved, or sick, they would come in and surrender, and get fed up and looked after until well again, when they would take the first opportunity of breaking away and making a fresh start.

CHAPTER X

BY ORDER--"NO QUARTER!"

Upon arrival at Fort Edward on Sunday morning, we learned that a convoy had arrived the previous day from Pietersburg, in charge of Lieutenant Neel--just in time to assist Captain Taylor and the few men who had been left in driving back a strong force of Boers who had come up close to the fort. There had been some sharp fighting, one Carbineer had been wounded, and several horses shot. It was here that Captain Taylor shot a Kaffir for refusing to give him information regarding the movements of the Boers, for which act later on he was tried and acquitted.

Lieutenant Neel remained at the fort for some days, and upon his return to Pietersburg was accompanied by Lieutenant Picton, who reported to the commanding officer and also to the commandant the whole of the facts regarding the shooting of Visser. No action was taken, not even a notice or message was sent intimating that such practices were to be discontinued. This tended to convince me that the orders and the interpretation of the orders regarding prisoners as transmitted to me by Lieutenant Morant were authentic, and that such proceedings were not only permitted, but were approved of by the headquarters authorities.

After our return to the fort, it was decided to send a small detachment of the Carbineers to occupy and work round Reuter's Mission Station. I asked Lieutenant Morant to send me in charge, but he ultimately sent Lieutenant Hannam, as he said I was not sufficiently acquainted with the district. He added that in a month he would recall Hannam and send me in his place.

Lieutenant Hannam captured a large number of prisoners and sent them in to Fort Edward. I can explain here how those infamous rumours gained currency as to the shooting of children by the Carbineers. A patrol of Lieutenant Hannam's men were out making a reconnaissance, when they suddenly came upon a Boer laager and opened fire. They heard women and children screathing, and ceased firing. Upon taking the laager they found that a child had been shot and two little girls slightly wounded.

I afterwards escorted these prisoners to Pietersburg, and in conversation with the parents of the children they told me that they in no way reproached Lieutenant Hannam or his men for what had happened; they were themselves to blame for running away from their waggons when called upon to surrender. This is the only foundation for the wicked reports as to the wholesale shooting of women and children by the Carbineers.

The day following Lieutenant Hannam's departure to the Mission Station, which was the 22nd August, a report reached Fort Edward that eight prisoners were being brought in. On the following morning Lieutenant Morant came to me and requested me to accompany him on patrol.

A patrol subsequently set out, consisting of Lieutenants Morant, Handcock, and myself, Sergeant-Major Hammett (who had gone out with me to the Spelonken), and two troopers. We first called at the office of Captain Taylor. Morant dismounted and had a private interview with that officer; I was not informed as to the nature of it. I was not then on intimate terms with Lieutenant Morant; I had only met him for the first time a fortnight previously as my superior officer, and had recognised him as such, and during that fortnight I had been frequently away from the fort.

We went on, and Morant said that it was his intention to have the prisoners shot. Both myself and Sergeant-Major Hammett asked Morant if he was sure he was doing right. He replied that he was quite justified in shooting the Boers; he had his orders, and he would rely upon us to obey him. I also afterwards remonstrated with him for having the prisoners brought in and shot so close to the fort, but he said it was a matter of indifference where they were shot.

We met the patrol with the prisoners about six miles out. Morant at once took charge, and instructed the escort to go on ahead as advance guard. The prisoners were ordered to inspan and trek on to the fort. I rode on in front of the waggon, and I did not see any civilian speak to the prisoners as we were passing the mission hospital. When we had trekked on about three miles Morant stopped the waggon, called the men off the road, and questioned them. Upon his asking, "Have you any more information to give?" they were shot. One of them, a big, powerful Dutchman, made a rush at me and seized the end of my rifle, with the intention of taking it and shooting me, but I simplified matters by pulling the trigger and shooting him. I never had any qualms of conscience for having done so, as he was recognised by Ledeboer, the intelligence agent, as a most notorious scoundrel who had previously threatened to shoot him, and was the head of a band of marauders. By just escaping death in this tragedy I was afterwards sentenced to suffer death.

I went on with the men, and we took with us the waggon and belongings, which we handed over to Captain Taylor. I then went on to the fort. Morant and Handcock remained behind to make arrangements for the burial of the bodies. About an hour afterwards Morant came in; a few minutes later he noticed a hooded buggy drawn by a pair of mules coming along the road at the foot of the fort, and going in the direction of Pietersburg. He immediately jumped on a horse, and rode down to see who it was, as no one was allowed to travel about the country without first getting permission to do so. When he returned he informed me that it was a missionary from Potgeiter's Rust returning home, and that he held a pass signed by Captain Taylor. Morant said that he had advised the missionary to wait until a convoy returned to Pietersburg, but he decided that he would go on alone. Morant then went away to see Captain Taylor. In the meantime Lieutenant Handcock returned, had his breakfast, and also went away again.

I have no idea of their subsequent movements, for being tired out I went to my bungalow, and slept until lunch time. I lunched alone, which was not unusual, but Morant and Handcock returned in the evening for dinner. During this repast the guard reported that rockets were being sent up in the direction of Bristow's farm, about one mile away. Morant took them for distress signals, and ordered the troops to stand to arms. Within twenty minutes a patrol of forty mounted men had the farm-house surrounded, but, much to the chagrin of Morant, it was found that the "signals" were a few rockets that had been thoughtlessly let off to amuse the children at the farm.

Nearly a week later, I, with Lieutenant Morant, was at Captain Taylor's office, when a neighbour came in and said there was a rumour abroad that a missionary had been killed on the road at Bandolier Kopjes, about 15 miles from Fort Edward, the most dangerous spot on the road to Pietersburg. I at once volunteered to take out a patrol and investigate. I was not permitted to go as far as Bandolier Kopjes, but was sent with half a dozen men to a farm-house five miles out to get what information I could, and was given orders by Lieutenant Morant not to go any further. Upon arrival at the farm I could glean nothing. I had all the natives brought up and questioned, but they did not know anything. I then went along the road to several kraals, but could get no news; I met a native post-boy with the mails from Pietersburg, and questioned him, but he knew nothing and had seen nothing along the road.

I then returned to the Fort, and on the way back met Taylor and Morant. I informed them of my inability to get any further information, and expressed to them my opinion that it was only a Kaffir yarn.

Two days later, however, Lieutenant Handcock was sent out to Bandolier Kopjes with a strong patrol to make a further search, and discovered the body of the missionary, his buggy, and his mules, some distance off the road. There was every indication that he had met his death by foul play. He had been shot in the breast, probably whilst sitting in his buggy; the mules, taking fright, had galloped off the road, throwing the missionary out as they travelled along. The buggy was found jammed between some trees and a telegraph post, with the pole broken. The mules had freed themselves, and were feeding about harnessed together. Lieutenant Handcock made arrangements for the burial of the missionary, and returned to the Fort, taking the mules with him.

Much of my work while at Fort Edward consisted of escorting convoys with prisoners and refugees, who were being sent into the concentration camps at Pietersburg. I took them half way, and then handed them over to a patrol sent out from Pietersburg. During these trips I came in contact with many of the "Boers of the Veldt," or the Dopper class. I would often take a cup of coffee with them, and as many of them could speak a little English, they would pour out all their troubles to me. The women folk were eager to learn all about the refugee camp, asking would they be provided with food and clothing, and would the "Englisher" "give them schoens for the kinder?" This is the class of people that predominates in South Africa, and in my opinion there must be generations of purging, educating, and civilising before they will be capable of taking part in national life. They appear habitually to shun water, and never undress; as they go to bed, so they get up again--dirty, untidy, and unwashed.

On one of these trips I became acquainted with a Dutchman who was employed by us as a transport rider. He had been fighting for his country at the outbreak of the war, but, tiring of it, had surrendered, and was afterwards employed by the Army Service Corps. In recounting his experience, he said that when he was first called out on commando he thought the war would only last a couple of months, as they would soon drive every Englishman out of the country. When leaving home he had promised his children that when he returned he would take them back a "little Englisher," which they could keep in a box, and feed on mealies and oats.

After the first great reverses, this man and many more would have surrendered but for the lying statements made to them by their predikants and commandants, who would harangue them from a trek waggon with statements that thousands of English had been repulsed and driven into the sea; that foreign powers had sent assistance and had already landed; that the Boers' homes had been desolated, and that their wives and daughters in the refugee camps were being outraged, and distributed amongst the soldiers with their daily issue of rations. The effect of these speeches was to make the men fight on more doggedly and bitterly than ever, and it is not wonderful that the rules and customs of civilised war were sometimes departed from.

The same man also told me that Kruger owed him #500 for the time he had been fighting with the Boers, and for the use of his waggon and oxen, and he asked me if I thought the English Government would pay him this amount.

Much has been said and written regarding the concentration camps and their management. I was in personal contact with some of the people who went into them, and I am certain that these, at least, were never as well off before as when there. It was stated that unsanitary conditions existed, and I can sympathise with the people who tried to make those conditions better. The task would be, I think, an impossible one, as most of the camp inmates had lived all their lives without even knowing what sanitation or cleanliness meant. Perhaps the mortality amongst children was greater in the camps than on the farms, especially if an epidemic of measles or diphtheria occurred, as the children mixed more with each other, and it would be difficult to isolate all cases; or perhaps there were more opportunities for a death to excite attention than there would be on a farm far out on the veldt. The majority of the inmates looked upon camp-life as a picnic. A few who had lived a sort of gipsy life previously were discontented, and anxious to start roving again; otherwise there was no cause for complaint.

CHAPTER XI

MORANT'S CREDITABLE EXPLOIT

About a fortnight after the finding of the body of the missionary, and while I was away from Fort Edward on convoy escort, three armed Boers were reported coming in. Upon Lieutenant Morant being informed, he went out, taking with him Lieutenant Handcock and two men. These Boers were met and shot.

The same day Major Lenehan arrived at Fort Edward from Pietersburg; he found the merry-hearted Morant, whom he had known for a number of years, a changed man. He was now gloomy and morose, and was still brooding over the manner of the death of Captain Hunt. Morant fancied that if he had been out with Hunt it would not have happened. The major thought, as did others, that Morant's mind had become unhinged with grief.

When I returned from Pietersburg, about two days later, I learned that two strong forces of Boers were reported in the district, and the outlook at Fort Edward was not a bright one.

Field-Cornet Torn Kelly, a notorious Boer Irregular leader, and a great fighter, was moving in from the Portuguese territory, and it was reported that he had several guns with him. Commandant Beyers, with a strong force, was threatening on another side. Morant had been wishing for months for a chance to capture Tom Kelly, and he now entreated Major Lenehan to allow him to go in pursuit. The major hesitated for some time, but finally gave permission to go. This brightened Morant up considerably.

On Monday, 16th September, Morant and myself left the Fort with thirty men in search of Kelly, proceeding in the direction of the Birthday Mine. We arrived there three days later, and waited for the scouts to come in and report the locality of Kelly's laager. Early on Saturday morning we started off again. Owing to the rough nature of the country we would have to travel over, we decided to leave behind all stores, taking with us only two days' rations, intending to live after that on any game we could shoot. Pushing on, we reached Banniella's (Kaffir) Kraal, within two miles of Kelly's laager, and about 150 miles from Fort Edward, late on Sunday evening. We dismounted, and left our horses here. The natives in formed us that Kelly had been there that day drinking palm wine with them, and had only left a couple of hours before; he had told them that if a thousand Englishmen came to his laager he would wipe them all out.

After warning the natives under penalty of death not to move away from the kraal, we proceeded on foot to the laager, which we reached at midnight. The camp was situated in a small clearing, among dense scrub, on the bank of the Thsombo River, and close to the Portuguese border. Halting within 300 yards of it, Morant and an intelligence agent named Constanteon made a careful reconnaisance, leaving me in charge of the men, some of whom were so fatigued that they almost immediately fell asleep.

One man, hearing a noise in the bush and leaves rustling, reported to me that he had seen a lion, and asked if he could shoot it. I knew that if we were successful in securing the lion we would lose Kelly, so I peremptorily ordered him to preserve strict silence until the laager was taken.

Morant returned shortly after, having found out the exact situation of the waggons and surroundings. He divided the patrol into three parties, and posted one on the right flank with Serjeant-Major Hammett, about 150 yards off; he and I took the others into the river bed, which ran under a steep bank around the waggons. The night was intensely cold, but we lay there within 50 yards of them until the first streak of dawn. During the night a dog scented us and started to bark; a Boer got up and gave it a kick to quieten it, at which Morant remarked, "A man never knows his luck in South Africa."

About four o'clock a Kaffir got up and lit a fire to make early morning coffee. We then charged the camp, shouting "Hands up" in the nearest approach to Dutch at our command. The Boers were taken completely by surprise. As there were women there we refrained from shooting. Morant rushed to Kelly's tent, and called upon him to surrender, and when he showed his head through the doorway he was looking straight down the barrel of Morant's rifle. The others, as they rolled from under the waggons, put up their hands very sulkily, while we collected the rifles.

Kelly was a fine type of a man, over six feet in height, and about 55 years of age; his father was an Irishman and his mother a Dutch woman. When I saw him again he was sitting in a Boer chair beside the fire; it had completely staggered him to realise that he was a prisoner, he who had boasted so often that he would give every Englishman a warm reception who came after him, and he had been taken without an opportunity of making the slightest resistance. The talk about the guns was all bluff. One of our troopers went up and asked him, "Where are the big guns?" He replied, snappishly, "Don't talk to me, young man, I'm a prisoner."

After collecting all the prisoners, we got together all the arms and ammunition, which were nearly all British, and sent a party back to the kraal for the horses. We then spanned in the oxen, and started on our return journey to Fort Edward. As the country was very rough, and there were no roads, it took us four days to get back to the Birthday Mine. When we outspanned on the third night the horse-guard reported several horses missing. My own spare horse being amongst them, on the following morning I left the convoy and returned with three men to the site of the previous outspan, and after scouring the country all day found the missing horses. We got back late the same night to the place we had started from in the morning; we had used up all our rations, and had been living for the last four days on what we could shoot in the way of game. Leaving before daylight, we reached the Birthday Mine about 10 a.m.; finding the caretaker at home, four hungry men made great havoc upon his stock of provisions, besides commandeering his mealies for our horses. After a short rest we hurried on to overtake the convoy, which we came up with late in the evening, having travelled 60 miles since morning; the last 70 miles was covered in two days, as we feared that Commandant Beyers, who was in the district, would try to intercept us.

Our rate of travelling with ox teams surprised the Dutchmen. Ten miles a day is their average trek, so that 35 and 40 miles a day was naturally regarded by them as a "bi goed trek" (very great trek).

When we arrived at Fort Edward two of Kelly's daughters left the waggon. I asked them where they were going. They replied, "Home to get the house ready"--not knowing that their home was now a heap of ruins. I could not tell them, as I knew the effect it would have on them.

After fighting in the earlier stages of the war, Commandant Kelly had returned to his farm, which was situated about half a mile from Fort Edward. As soon as the Carbineers went to the district, he went off again on trek with his family rather than surrender. There were a number of other farmers living quietly around there. They had been frequently visited by Boer commandos, and all their horses and mealies or maize corn that could be found had been commandeered.

From the time we left in search of Kelly to our return to Fort Edward was exactly a fortnight; his pursuit and capture was the last official military duty of Lieutenant Morant. He received the following message from Colonel Hall:--"Very glad to hear of your success, and should like to have an account of what must have been a good bit of work."

Morant's career in South Africa was adorned by not a few actions such as this, but accounts of them were never published broadcast to his credit, to balance the stories scattered to his detriment.

After handing over Kelly's commando intact to the Pietersburg authorities, Morant was granted a fortnight's leave, and went to Pretoria. Just about this time Captain Taylor was recalled. Three weeks later Morant's detachment was relieved at Fort Edward, and returned to Pietersburg. On 21st October Major Lenehan, myself, Lieutenant Handcock, and all non-commissioned officers and men who had been on service in the district left Spelonken, and arrived at Fort Klipdan, 15 miles out of Pietersburg, on the evening of the 22nd.

The following morning we made an eventful entry into the garrison. I was riding ahead with the advance guard, and when about three miles from the town I was met by two mounted officers, who inquired if I was Lieutenant Witton. Upon replying in the affirmative, they informed me that the garrison commandant wished to see me. One of the officers accompanied me into Pietersburg, and took me direct to the commandant's office, where I met Major Neatson, staff officer to Colonel Hall, who merely asked me if I was Lieutenant Witton. Upon replying again in the affirmative, he gave the officer who accompanied me some instructions. Leaving the commandant's office, I was requested to accompany him to the Garrison Artillery Fort. The proceedings seemed rather strange to me, as I had not the slightest conception of what was about to take place. On my arrival at the fort I was left with Lieutenant Beattie, who could not or would not enlighten me. A little later Major Neatson came to me and informed me that I was under close arrest pending a court of inquiry.

The officer commanding the fort then informed me that I was a military prisoner under his charge, and if I attempted to escape, or went outside the wire entanglements, I would be shot; that I was not to communicate with anyone outside, and all correspondence was to be sent through him. At this time I had not the faintest notion of the charges against me, or for what reason I was made a prisoner.

I learned afterwards that Major Lenehan, Captain Taylor, Lieutenants Morant, Handcock, Picton, Hannam, and Sergeant-Major Hammett were in the same predicament as myself, and were located in different parts of the garrison. Major Lenehan was with the 2nd Wiltshire Regiment, Captain Taylor and Lieutenant Handcock in blockhouses close to the Wiltshire lines, Lieutenant Hannam and Sergeant-Major Hammett at the garrison prison, Lieutenant Picton with the Royal Field Artillery, Lieutenant Morant first with the Gordon Highlanders, and afterwards at the garrison prison.

After being a fortnight in close confinement I was called upon to attend a sitting of the court of inquiry, and for the first time I became aware of the nature of the charges against me. A great deal of pride is evinced in what is called British justice, but after that court of inquiry I doubted if such a thing existed. This piece of history could well be dated back to the days of the Star Chamber or the Spanish Inquisition.

59

The president of the court appeared to be Colonel Carter, whilst Captain Evans acted as his secretary. Both belonged to the Wiltshire Regiment. There was also another member, belonging to the same regiment. He was constituted a sort of private detective to round up witnesses to give evidence to meet necessary requirements; he employed as an understrapper a corporal who had once been a South African Republic detective, and was afterwards a trooper in the Carbineers. He had been arrested several times whilst with the corps, and on one occasion was reprimanded for selling British uniform. He expected at the close of the case to be rewarded with a farm. His hostility and bitterness can be imagined when be openly boasted that he would be willing to walk barefooted from Spelonken to Pietersburg, 90 miles, to be in a firing party to shoot Morant and Handcock.

Upon my appearance at the court, which was held in a tent close to the commandant's office, the president read out that I was charged with complicity in the death of a prisoner of war named Visser, with complicity in the death of eight others, names unknown, also with complicity in the death of C. H. D. Hesse, a German missionary.

I was asked to make a statement regarding these charges. I said that any part I had taken in the shooting of Boers was under the direct orders of a superior officer; as to the death of the missionary, it was quite a mystery to me, but I was confident that it could not be charged to the Carbineers.

I was astounded to hear that his death was imputed to Lieutenant Handcock, as I had been frequently in his company while at Spelonken, and had not the slightest reason to connect him with it. I proved even to the satisfaction of that court that I knew nothing of this case, and the charge was immediately withdrawn.

I always understood that a man was innocent until he was proved to be guilty; that position was here reversed, and we were adjudged guilty until we proved we were innocent.

CHAPTER XII

ORDERED FOR COURT-MARTIAL

It appears that the ground for these remarkable proceedings was that a report, which had originated through a Kaffir boy, had reached the German authorities that a subject of theirs had been shot by British troops. Redress was demanded, a penalty must be paid, and the result was the arrest of the officers of the Carbineers as stated.

It has been said that the missionary was shot because he was going into Pietersburg to inform the authorities there about the shooting of prisoners, but there was no necessity to shoot him on that account, as the authorities there were aware of the facts.

It was customary in outlying districts during the latter stages of the war to shoot as many of the enemy as possible. Vaguely-worded orders were issued that "All officers should strive to the utmost to bring the war to a speedy termination;" "All officers must use discretion in dealing with the white flag;" or, as one officer said, he was told to "clear the district, and not to be too keen on filling burgher camps." These orders were interpreted in only one way by the officers, and that was "No quarter, no prisoners."

On the morning I attended a sitting of the court a German farmer from near Duival's Kloof, who was alleged to have seen the body of Captain Hunt, was being examined. "Did you notice any marks on his face?" he was asked, "There was a graze over his eye, which might have been caused by coming in contact with the branch of a tree at night time," was the reply. "Did you notice any extravasation of blood about the neck?" I could see the man did not know what was meant by extravasation of blood, but he replied in the negative. "In your opinion, then, Captain Hunt's body had not been maltreated ?" "Yes."

It is reasonable to conclude that this man, being a German, would be a biassed witness, and, again, that he would not dare to give evidence favourable to British troops, as his farm and possessions were at the mercy of every Boer commando that came into the district. Notwithstanding this, I shall prove later that this man's evidence-- taken at this court, and not at the court-martial--was accepted as correct, as against that given by a clergyman and a British officer.

When the men of the Carbineers were being examined they were questioned in a most high-handed manner, and in some cases questions and answers would be taken down in writing without their knowledge; a day or so later they would be sent for again, and a long statement read over to them, which they were ordered to sign. Some of the statements were made by men who knew nothing whatever personally, but had only heard the case was as they represented; some even had merely heard that someone else had heard, and so on. These men's statements were taken as evidence. Others who were called, and said truly that they knew nothing, were treated as hostile, and were bullied and badgered, and even threatened with arrest. One man was actually sent to the garrison prison, and detained there until he was removed to the hospital suffering from brain fever.

In addition to the men of our own regiment, evidence was taken from Dutchmen, Germans, Africanders, and Kaffirs.

When Lieutenant Handcock was brought before the court he was staggered at the charges laid against him; it seemed as if he were charged with the murder of every Dutchman that had been shot in South Africa, as well as that of a German missionary. He was so completely ignorant of military law and court proceedings that he asked the president what would be the best course for him to pursue; he was advised to make a clean breast of everything, as the responsibility would rest solely on Lieutenant Morant. He declined to make any statement whatsoever, and was sent again for a considerable time into close confinement, even the military chaplain not being allowed to see him.

Is it possible to conceive such an iniquity perpetrated in these days of supposed civilisation?--a man charged with numerous murders shut up alone, without a soul from whom he could seek advice; condemned before he was tried. There could be only one ending; Handcock's mind gave way, and when he was not responsible for his actions he was forced into making a statement which incriminated himself and Lieutenant Morant.

This court of inquisition sat daily for nearly a month, and was supposed to be held in camera, yet statements made during the day, with additions, were freely discussed at garrison mess, and were the common talk of the town during the evening.

Captain Taylor's charge-sheet was, I believe, a notable one, and almost identical with that of Lieutenant Handcock--if not for the actual crimes, for instigating them. The statements made by some of his men would, I am sure, furnish interesting reading; the majority of the charges against him were, however, withdrawn.

After twelve weeks' solitary confinement Handcock was allowed to make arrangements for his defence. Upon being made aware of his position by his friends, he refuted his previous statement, and said that he had only made it to please Colonel Carter; it was too late then, however, as I was informed on good authority that a copy of the evidence taken at the court had been furnished to the German Government.

With me, who was also kept in solitary confinement, time just passed on; I waited, wondering what the future would bring forth. I was in no way worried, because I could not think that I was in any way culpable for what had happened in the Spelonken district. Towards the end of December I was again requested to attend a sitting of the court of inquiry; on this occasion Lieutenants Morant, Handcock, and Picton were present.

Morant appeared gloomy and irritable. The past months of close confinement had greatly impaired his health, physically and mentally, and he looked upon current events from a very pessimistic standpoint; Handcock was even more silent than usual, and looked much worried and dejected.

We were informed by the president that we would be tried by court-martial at an early date, and the statements of the witnesses for the prosecution were read over to us. Morant listened in austere silence to the end, then, springing to his feet, exclaimed, "Look here, Colonel, you have got us all here now; take us out and crucify us at once, for as sure as God made pippins, if you let one man off he'll yap."

The following afternoon I attended the court to hand in names of witnesses I required for my defence. I requested to be allowed to ascertain if Mr. Rail, of Capetown, would act as prisoner's friend or counsel for me at the forthcoming trial. Captain Evans was there alone; he was considered the best authority on military law in the garrison, and no one could have a better grasp of the case than he, as he had attended every sitting of the court as secretary. In conversation with him in regard to obtaining counsel and witnesses, he informed me that he had gone into my case thoroughly, and he considered that I had taken such a subordinate part that it was not necessary for me to go to the trouble of bringing counsel or witnesses from Capetown. "You have nothing to fear or trouble about," he said, "you are bound to be exonerated." Confident of a speedy and honourable acquittal, I made no further efforts for my defence.

Shortly after the conclusion of the court of inquiry the Bushveldt Carbineers Regiment was disbanded. Men who were required as witnesses for the prosecution were given their discharges and as much as #1 per day detention allowance to remain in Pietersburg. The remainder were discharged and sent out of the district, as though purposely to obstruct the course of justice, and when certain men, most important witnesses for the defence, were asked for, the authorities at first refused to make any inquiries as to their whereabouts, and stated that the expense of securing their return would have to be borne by the defence. This was acquiesced in, and later on the authorities declared that they were unable to trace the men asked for. Yet at this very time a witness most important to me was travelling by permission of the Pretoria authorities on the Pietersburg line, and had just visited Nylstroom.

On the 15th January, just twelve weeks from the date of my arrest, I was served with the charge-sheets.

Case one was that I did when on active service commit murder by inciting, instigating, and commanding certain troopers to kill and murder one named Visser. Case two was that when on active service I committed the offence of murder by inciting, instigating, and commanding certain troopers to kill and murder eight men, names unknown. I was warned to appear at a general court-martial at 9 o'clock the following morning. I was then granted the liberty, under proper escort, to visit or be visited by any of the other prisoners.

I went straight to Lieutenant Morant, and asked him if he knew anything about a court-martial, or had taken any steps towards a defence. Producing my charge-sheets, I informed him that I was charged with nine murders. "Only nine!" he ejaculated, "that is nothing; I am charged with twelve, and an infanticide." The last three prisoners shot by him had been entered in his charge-sheet as two men and a boy. The "boy" was about 18 or 20, and had been right through the war and seen more active service than many a veteran soldier, or than nine-tenths of the Carbineers. This was the first time I had spoken to Lieutenant Morant since my arrest.

I then learned that Major Thomas, a member of the New South Wales Mounted Rifles, and an Australian solicitor, whom Major Lenehan had secured to undertake his own defence, would act for us all. I was unable to interview Major Thomas, who had arrived that morning, as he was all day closeted with Major Lenehan. The following morning, about 8.30 o'clock, he paid me a hurried visit, which lasted for a few minutes only. In this time I briefly detailed to him the part I had been compelled to take, which had resulted in the charges now preferred against me. I was then escorted to the court-house in the town.

Court-martial held at Pietersburg, Transvaal, on the 16th day of January, 1902, by order of Lord Kitchener of Khartoum, commanding the forces of South Africa. The court was constituted as follows:-- The president was Lieutenant-Colonel Denny, 2nd Northampton Regiment. The members were Brevet-Major J. Little, same regiment; Brevet-Major Thomas and Major Ousely, of the Royal Field Artillery; Captain Brown, of the 2nd Wiltshire Regiment; Captain Marshall, 1st Gordon Highlanders; Captain Nicholson, 1st Cameron Highlanders. Waiting members: Captain Matcham, 2nd Wiltshire Regiment; Captain Jobson, Royal Garrison Artillery. Major C. S. Copeland, 2nd

Northampton Regiment, acted as Judge Advocate; Captain Bums-Begg as Crown Prosecutor. Major Thomas, New South Wales Mounted Rifles, was counsel for prisoners.

After the preliminary proceedings of the court and the swearing of the members, an adjournment was made until the following morning to enable a telegram to be sent to headquarters asking authority for Major Thomas to undertake our defence.

The necessary authority being obtained, the court assembled the following morning, and the first charge, that of murdering a prisoner named Visser, was proceeded with. On the plea of "Not guilty," witnesses for the prosecution were called. These described the fight at Duival's Kloof, and how Captain Hunt was killed, and the state of his body when found, and also gave particulars as to the capture of Visser, who was wearing portion of Captain Hunt's clothing.

An intelligence agent named Ledeboer deposed that he informed Visser of his position, and that he was condemned to be shot. Upon being cross-examined, several of the witnesses stated that Captain Hunt had previously given them orders not to take prisoners, and they had been reprimanded for bringing them in.

For the defence, Lieutenant Morant stated that he had been under Captain Hunt, clearing the northern district of Boers. It was regular guerilla warfare; Captain Hunt acted on orders he got in Pretoria, which were in effect to clear Spelonken and take no prisoners. Captain Hunt had told him that Colonel Hamilton, military secretary, had given him the orders at Lord Kitchener's private house where he had gone with a pair of polo ponies, just prior to his departure for Spelonken. All the detachment knew of the order given by Captain Hunt not to bring in prisoners. After the death of Captain Hunt he took command and went out with reinforcements, and when he learned the circumstances of his death, and how he had been maltreated, he told the others that he had previously disregarded the orders of Captain Hunt, but in future he would carry them out, as he considered they were lawful. The orders had only been transmitted verbally by Captain Hunt, and he had quoted the actions of Kitchener's Horse and Strathcona's Horse as precedents; he never questioned the validity of the orders, he was certain they were correct. He had shot no prisoner before Visser, and the

66

facts in Visser's case had been reported to Captain Taylor, also to Major Lenehan and Colonel Hall.

"Was your court at the trial of Visser constituted like this?" asked the President, "and did you observe paragraph ---- of ---- section of the King's Regulations?" "Was it like this!" fiercely answered Morant. "No; it was not quite so handsome. As to rules and sections, we had no Red Book, and knew nothing about them. We were out fighting the Boers, not sitting comfortably behind barb-wire entanglements; we got them and shot them under Rule 303."

Morant made a plucky defence; he openly admitted the charges, and took all responsibility upon himself, pleading custom of the war and orders from headquarters. He did not express any regret, or have any fear as to what his fate might be. Driven almost to desperation, and smarting under the recent unjust acts of the court of inquiry, he, in his usual hot-headed manner, made disclosures which he believed would in all probability "stagger humanity." He vowed that he would have Lord Kitchener put into the box and cross-examined as to the orders given to officers, and his methods of conducting the war. The folly of all this was apparent to everyone, as Lord Kitchener held Morant's life in his hands; but Morant would not be restrained, and was prepared to suffer.

Lieutenant Picton was the next witness called for the defence. He had served in the war for two years, and had gained a distinguished conduct medal. He had commanded the firing party that had shot Visser, and had carried out the execution in obedience to Morant's orders. He had reported the matter to Major Lenehan and Colonel Hall. He also had received orders from Captain Hunt not to take prisoners.

Lieutenant Handcock corroborated previous evidence as to the reasons for executing Visser, and also as to the orders not to take prisoners. I also supported the evidence as to the information received from the Rev. F. L. Reuter about the maltreatment of Captain Hunt.

The Rev. F. L. Reuter, missionary, deposed that the bodies of Captain Hunt and Sergeant Eland were brought to his place; that of the late Captain Hunt was much mutilated. The neck appeared to have been broken, and the face bore marks of boot-heels, and was much bruised; the body had been stripped, and the legs gashed.

Dr. Johnson testified that he was of opinion from the evidence that the injuries to Captain Hunt's body had been caused before death.

Captain Taylor stated that he had received messages from the Boers through natives that if he fell into their hands he would be given four days to die, which meant that they would torture him, because he was known to them. The Boers in that part did not form part of a legal commando, but were rather outlaws. Major Lenehan gave evidence that Picton had reported the shooting of Visser to him, and he had reported it to Colonel Hall.

CHAPTER XIII

BEYERS--AND THE FLAG HE SLEPT ON

When Morant's detachment was withdrawn from Spelonken, and the officers arrested, the Boers returned to the district, full of renewed hope; they were well acquainted with the fighting abilities of our successors. The war had been going on for so long that even in those out-of-the-way places, both sides were as well-known to each other as rivals for party power would be in the snug quarters of Parliament House, or even as rival factions in a little country township, where the causes for tumult are numerous and varied.

In December Commandant Beyers, with a strong force, fairly beleagured Fort Edward, billeting himself and his men at Sweetwater's Farm, about a mile away, in the quarters recently vacated by Captain Taylor. Beyers had occupied the same place about nine months before, but when the Carbineers appeared upon the scene he went elsewhere.

Just before his first visit the good lady of the house had made a large Union Jack in anticipation of the advent of the Carbineers. She knew that if it fell into the hands of the Dutchmen it would not only go hard with the flag, but with the homestead as well. She was determined it should not be destroyed, and a happy thought struck her; she wrapped it carefully round a pillow, and enclosed it in two pillow cases, one reverse to the other, and placed it on the bed in which Beyers slept, so that nightly he rested his head comfortably on the grand old

Union Jack. The flag was preserved, and for many months afterwards it fluttered nobly in the breeze at Fort Edward.

For nearly a fortnight Beyers and his men stayed at the farm, moving about among the settlers, helping themselves to the cattle and doing what they pleased, and passing many a joke at the expense of the Fort Edward garrison, who all this time were penned up and not allowed to move outside the walls.

The men entreated the officers to take them out and engage Beyers, and were almost on the verge of mutiny through the inaction of their leaders, when reinforcements, including a detachment of the Field Artillery, arrived from Pietersburg. Then, and only then, were the occupants of Fort Edward permitted to move outside.

On the approach of the troops Beyers and his force fled in the direction of the Waterberg, hotly pursued by the Carbineers, who several times came in touch with them, and exchanged a few shots. In one of these engagements the horse of Beyers' adjutant was shot under him, and he was captured. He appeared to be of the better class of Dutchman, and a well-informed man. He freely spoke of the tight way in which the Spelonken district had been held under the military rigime of Lieutenant Morant, and said that the men of Beyers' commando absolutely refused to work in that district until they learned of Morant's removal and arrest, when they ventured back.

Beyers now turned his attention to Pietersburg. During the trial of the Visser case, on the night of the 22nd January, the soldiers who were in the blockhouses guarding the camp were enticed from their duty by the Boer women. Beyers, with a strong force, then rushed the Burgher camp, and, unchallenged, entered it, looted a quantity of provisions, and took away 150 men who had previously surrendered and had been allowed to remain with their families in the camp.

Upon an inquiry being made into the conduct of the soldiers on guard, several were court-martialled and sentenced to terms of imprisonment ranging from six months to two years.

It was anticipated that the Boers, having secured a large number of recruits, would require remounts and equipment, so on the following day arms were returned to the late officers of the Carbineers, and we were ordered to be ready for duty when called upon. Next morning, just as the day was breaking, the Boer force rushed upon the town, making for the Remount Depot. This necessitated breaking through the ring of block-houses at the point where Handcock was confined, and close to the garrison prison where Morant was located. From my position near the cow-gun I saw the Boers galloping madly over the sky-line, making for the town, doubtless thinking that the forts were only dummies and unoccupied, and expecting to annex the remounts as easily as they had the recruits.

They were allowed to come within fifty yards of the block-houses, when they received a warm welcome from within in the shape of a shower of bullets. They made a desperate effort even then to get through, firing as they charged. Handcock was at the block-house nearest the point of attack. This had originally been a small brick building, and had been converted into a fort by being loop-holed and sangered.

Morant joined Handcock as soon as the firing commenced, and they climbed together on to the flat roof of the fort, in the most exposed position. Disregarding any cover, they fought as only such brave and fearless men can fight. Handcock in particular, in his cool and silent manner, did splendid work, one of his bullets finding its billet in Marthinus Pretorius, Beyers' fighting leader. Handcock was the only man armed with a Mauser rifle, and when Pretorius was brought in, dangerously wounded, it was found that he had been struck by a Mauser bullet.

The Boers were repulsed, leaving many dead and wounded behind, some being within a few yards of the block-house. Whilst they were beating a hasty retreat in a north-easterly direction, I espied a party making round the foot of Krughersberg Kopje, about one mile and a-half from the fort. I drew the attention of the cow-gun officer to them, and he hurriedly had the gun loaded, and sent a 50-lb. lyddite shell after them. This resulted in a rather inopportune disaster that put the gun out of action until the Boers had got safely away. When loading the gun, the gunners, in their hurry and excitement, neglected to put the brake on the wheels to check the recoil; consequently the shock of discharge drove it back to the top of the inclined plane at the rear, then, running forward again, it took a header off the gun floor into a deep ditch, burying the muzzle in the ground, while the trail pointed in the direction of 10 on a clock--just the time for the court to assemble. It was fortunate that none of the gunners were killed; one man had his foot crushed by the gun running over it, and he was removed to the hospital. No casualties from the other side were reported.

Such a gun as that, in the hands of an inefficient officer, is a greater danger to those around him than it is to the enemy.

The court met as usual that day. The members were just a little more imperious; perhaps they were slightly tired by their exertions in the early morning. During the day the Pietersburg Light Horse, a corps formed in place of the now defunct Carbineers, went out under an Imperial officer in pursuit of Beyers, and with him went any late members of the Carbineers who had been detained in Pietersburg as witnesses at the trials.

They came in touch a short distance out, at a place called Matapanspoort; upon climbing a kopje and looking down on the other side, they saw Commandant Beyers dismounted and within 150 yards of them. A late member of the Carbineers at once covered him, and asked permission from the officer commanding to open fire, or at least to shoot Beyers' horse and capture him, but this request was refused until more men were got up from below. In the meantime, Beyers, with a party of his men within easy range, and the British troops looking idly on, was allowed to pass out through the Poort. A little time after his departure another party came riding in through the same pass. The commanding officer on the kopje was just about to order his men to open fire, when one of them discerned that the party approaching was some of their own men, who had been sent round on the flank. Just as I write this I can extract a cablegram published in the Melbourne "Age," and dated from London on 20th February, 1905, to the effect that at a recent conference of leading Transvaal Boers at Pietersburg "Ex-General Beyers made a violent speech, threatening that, if representative and responsible government were not immediately granted to the Transvaal, there would be a rebellion of Boers after the fashion of the Slaghter's Nek rising in the old days of Cape Colony." He still adheres to that deliverance, for a further cable said that, "In an interview at Potgietersrust yesterday, Beyers declared that he meant what he said at Pietersburg, and if a second Transvaal war should occur, the blame would be with the capitalists, who are the controllers of the present policy, and who are interested solely in the Rand mines."

I am wondering if Commandant Beyers is aware that he owes his life to the hesitancy of an English officer.

The court should have had a little rest that day, and sent Morant and Handcock after Beyers. A monument to his memory would then have been the only cross the Empire would have had to carry for him.

Morant had his favourite horse, "Bideford Boy," stabled at the garrison prison near him, claiming it as his private property; he kept it, too, in spite of the requests and demands of the commandant to hand it over to the Pietersburg Light Horse. He wrote this skit on the venture of the Pietersburg Light Horse and the English major who went out and essayed to capture Beyers:--

"A new foot-slogging Major has ventured out of town, To spoil the mouth of 'Bideford,' and break the pony down; But when he sallies after Boers, it's different now to then-- He's got to let the Dutchmen rip, to muster up his men."

CHAPTER XIV

FURTHER PROCEEDINGS OF COURT-MARTIAL

Next day the court adjourned to Pretoria to take the evidence of Colonel Hamilton, military secretary to Lord Kitchener. My escort (or "tug-boat," as these individuals were termed in nautical phraseology by Lieutenant Morant) was a newly-commissioned lieutenant in the Pietersburg Light Horse.

Fully armed and equipped, we proceeded by rail to Pretoria. Quarters were provided for all the prisoners at the Mounted Infantry Depot, about a mile from the town. The following day the court, which was constituted as at Pietersburg, assembled at the Artillery Barracks to take the evidence of Colonel Hamilton; all the prisoners were present, and when this officer appeared every eye was upon him. He was stern and hard-featured, and looked just then very gaunt and hollow-eyed, as though a whole world of care rested on his shoulders. He was apparently far more anxious than those whose fate depended on the evidence he was to give. The following is his evidence:--

Examined by the Court:--Lieut. Morant, in his evidence, states that the late Capt. Hunt told him that he had received orders from you that no prisoners were to be taken alive. Is this true?

Ans.: Absolutely untrue.

Examined by Counsel for Prisoners:--

Do you remember Captain Hunt taking two polo ponies early in July last up to Lord Kitchener's quarters;' at which time you came in, and had a conversation with Capt. Hunt?

Ans.: No. I have no recollection whatever. I have never spoken to Capt. Hunt with reference to his duties in the Northern Transvaal.

The Counsel for the Prisoners then made the following address:--As regards the evidence of Colonel Hamilton, just called, I wish to state that the defence do not regard his evidence, one way or the other, as having any real bearing on the defence; in fact, I submit to the court that it is really illegal evidence. It really amounts to this: A certain conversation is stated to have taken place between Colonel Hamilton and the deceased, Capt. Hunt, which conversation was mentioned by Capt. Hunt to Lieut. Morant, apparently in a confidential or private way. This, having been obtained by the court from the prisoner Morant, is then sought to be contradicted by the evidence of Colonel Hamilton, which, I submit, is quite contrary to the laws of evidence. It really does not matter much, from the point of view of the defence, where Capt. Hunt got his instructions. The fact is clear from the evidence that Capt. Hunt did tell his subordinates, not once, but many times, that prisoners were not to be taken. This fact is admitted by witnesses for the prosecution. The chief value of these instructions, as given by Capt. Hunt, is that they go to show that he, being a man of some standing, and a personal friend of Lieut. Morant, they were entitled to weight, and go to remove any question of malicious intent.

Now, the four prisoners are jointly charged with the crime of murder--not as principals, but as accessories before the fact. The principals, or actual perpetrators of the alleged murders, are four troopers named Silke, Thomson, Botha, and Honey, according to the indictment. As a matter of fact, the evidence for the prosecution shows that there were ten, and that they formed a firing party, which under orders shot Visser, the man alleged to be murdered. It is charged that the prisoners committed this offence, by wilfully, feloniously, and with malice aforethought, inciting, instigating, and commanding these four persons to kill and murder one Visser, and that the persons mentioned accordingly did kill and murder him. This should be borne clearly in mind all through the case, that these prisoners did not actually commit the murder, nor are they charged with such, but with instigating others to do it. Now, under the law, it is clear that he who instigates or procures another to commit a felony is himself liable to the same punishment as the actual felon. But persons charged with being accessories to the crime cannot be convicted as such unless the guilt of the principals be first established. Nobody can be an accessory to a crime which is not proven. Under the old Common Law of England it was absolutely necessary that before an accessory could be found guilty there should be an actual verdict of guilty against the principal, so that if the principal managed to evade justice the accessory escaped also. But under existing English law, I believe the accessory may now be tried and convicted, although the principal is not before the court, and has not been convicted but, I take it, it would be only in very special circumstances that this would be done, where it is absolutely impossible to obtain the principal, in order to bring him to justice. It seems proper that if we suppose one man instigates another to murder a third, and the murder takes place, and the actual murderer flies the country before trial, if the fact of the murder is clear and beyond all doubt, the accessory should not escape. But in this case all the alleged principals are easily obtainable, yet we find that not one of them is before the court, except that inferentially it is averred in the charge-sheet that they actually murdered Visser. If that is so, and they are murderers, why are not these four actual perpetrators charged before the court? However, be that as it may, this must be very clear to the court, that this court cannot convict the four prisoners of inciting, instigating, or commanding the four troopers to commit the murder, which murder it is alleged these four troopers actually committed, unless they are satisfied that the troopers are malicious and felonious murderers. The court must, therefore, I submit, clearly in its mind say these four troopers are murderers, who may now or at some future time be brought before a court of justice and tried for their lives as murderers. That is the extraordinary position in which the court finds itself, because these four troopers have merely been inferentially set down as murderers. They must be convinced on these two points:--

(1) That they are murderers.

(2) That the prisoners now before the court incited them to commit that murder.

If the court is not satisfied that they are men who should suffer death, the charge against the prisoners, as accessories, must fall to the ground.

Now, has the prosecution attempted to show that the murder was committed by these troopers? I submit the contrary. Two were brought as witnesses by the prosecution. They were not even warned to be careful lest they should incriminate themselves, and, really, I submit to the court that the assumption that these troopers are murderers is simply monstrous, and cannot by any possible means be substantiated. Clearly, they only obeyed the orders of a superior officer, and formed a firing party for the execution of Visser after their officers had held a summary court-martial and convicted him. There is not the slightest evidence that these troopers were in any way a party to the shooting of Visser, except that they obeyed their orders as soldiers. They are, therefore, not murderers. How can they be called such? If they are not murderers, there can be no accessories to the alleged crime. Even if the court-martial was improperly constructed, its proceedings informal, or its decision illegal, how could these four troopers, against none of whom there is any suggestion of crime, be regarded as murderers, simply because they fired the shots which killed Visser. The guilt of the four prisoners depends entirely upon the guilt of the four troopers. The troopers have been stigmatised as murderers, so as to found the charge against the four prisoners. If it was desired by the prosecution to shift home a malicious and unwarrantable act, resulting in the death of this man, it seems to me that the four prisoners should be charged with conspiring together to bring about the death of Visser by unlawful means. It should have been made a conspiracy amongst themselves, and the troopers should have been left out of it. Instead of which these men are called murderers.

Suppose these four troopers were now on trial and said they simply obeyed their orders, the court could not have convicted them, and I say that the charge, if any, against the prisoners should be a conspiracy amongst themselves to do an illegal act. Yet another difficulty arises when we come to deal with the prisoners individually. Lieutenant Morant, no doubt, is primarily responsible, being senior officer at the time when the trial took place, and the court has to be satisfied in his case, as in that of the others, that he deliberately and feloniously ordered the men to commit murder. There is no doubt that Captain Hunt did give certain very definite orders to Lieutenant Morant, and on his death Mr. Morant took over command. There is no doubt that his conduct was largely influenced by the treatment of the body of his friend, showing circumstances of barbarity, even if the injuries inflicted upon Captain Hunt, as clearly shown by Mr. Reuter's testimony, were done after death, although the medical evidence goes to show they were committed before death. There is no doubt that this did prompt him with the spirit of retaliation against the Boers who had done this thing. In war retaliation is justifiable, revenge is justifiable. Rules applicable in times of peace are quite inapplicable in times of war. In the Manual of Military Law it is stated, "Retaliation is military vengeance;" it takes place when an outrage committed on one side is avenged by a similar act on the other. I am free to admit that this maltreatment of his friend did exercise an influence over him when he came to deal with this man Visser, and it is natural he should be so influenced. He pursues these Boers, which ends in the capture of Visser, whom he finds wearing clothing the property of the late Captain Hunt. I go so far as saying that under the circumstances Mr. Morant would have been perfectly justified in shooting Visser straight away. The fact of wearing British uniform is altogether against the customs of war, and I know that this man Visser was present when Captain Hunt was killed from the evidence. At the request apparently, of Mr. Picton, it was decided to give Visser a court-martial--such a court-martial as is frequently held in the field, under the circumstances in which this was held. Informal, no doubt; how can we expect formality in the field, in the immediate vicinity of the enemy, and when Visser himself admitted that the Boers had promised to recapture him? All this is provided for in the Manual of Military Law. We claim that substantial justice was done, and I submit that there is nothing whatever to satisfy the court that Mr. Morant ordered a wilful or felonious murder. On the contrary, under the Rules of War, I consider that he was quite justified in confirming the sentence. The evidence of Captain Taylor shows that these men were the offshoots of commandoes and mere outlaws, who went about looting from Kaffirs, and, what I say now I wish to apply to all the prisoners. They were dealing in that particular district with a party of irresponsible outlaws, under no recognised control, sending in threats of torture, &c. In July, 1901, trains were wickedly wrecked, and numbers of men wounded. Such men forfeit all rights to be treated as prisoners of war. When irregulars are sent out to deal with an enemy of this kind, marauders and train wreckers, the officers should be allowed a wide discretion in dealing with them. If they err technically, or even make serious mistakes, they must be upheld. We cannot afford, in dealing with people of this description, to go into nice points of sentiment. I submit the irregular troops, sent out to deal with the people in this particular district, were entitled to deal with them as outlaws. I do not ask for proclamations to say we must do these sort of things, but we must take it for granted that we must do so. Departures from the usual customs of war have, in many instances, been visited by the troops by methods which they merit. No one denies that chivalric actions have been done by the Boers, but I say also that there are districts where that sort of thing does not occur at all, and notably in the particular district in which Visser was caught.

If the prisoners have been mistaken in their views as to what they were entitled to do, then it must be assumed that they erred in judgment; they may be even open to censure, but not charged with committing murder.

I claim from this court that the prisoners shall not be stigmatised as inciters to murder, because, acting on a responsibility which was naturally their own, they did carry out what I submit is only martial judgment. Lieutenant Picton undoubtedly gave the order to fire to the firing party, and in doing so simply obeyed his orders. Witton and Handcock simply, on being summoned to the court-martial, coincided with the views of their superior officer; further than this they took no place in the proceedings. They cannot be charged with inciting and instigating, even if they concurred in the verdict; the verdict was of no effect until confirmed by Mr. Morant.

I submit to the court that this charge is improperly made, or, if it is ostensibly correctly made, then it must fall to the ground, for the simple reason that this court cannot, I submit, say that the crime of murder against the troopers is proved to the court's satisfaction, and if that is not proved, then nobody can be found guilty of being accessory.

The Prosecutor replies:--

The defence has made a good deal of the fact that the court must hold the four troopers guilty of murder before they can hold the four prisoners now before them guilty of accessories. That is perfect nonsense. The Manual of Military Law says that where a person has been guilty of killing another the law presumes the killer to be guilty of murder (page 125), and on that the court must necessarily rest content, in so far as the guilt or innocence of the troopers is concerned. This is borne out by the statute law of England, which enables an accessory to be tried before, after, or with a principal felon, irrespective of the guilt or innocence of the latter.

The defence also raises the question, on the indictment, whether or not I have succeeded in proving that the prisoners each and all incited and commanded the troopers under their command to kill Visser. As regards that, I have no doubt the Judge Advocate will direct you that where a common criminal intent is proved to be shared by several persons, any criminal action by any one of these persons in furtherance of that criminal intent, may be visited on any one of them, and could any clearer proof of common intent be submitted than the prisoners' own description of what took place at the so-called court-martial. I thought that the prisoners would rely mainly on the alleged orders of Captain Hunt, and on this so-called court-martial for their defence. To the first contention I would point out, a complete answer is returned by the Manual of Military Law, which says that an officer is responsible for the carrying out of even lawful commands which result in injury, and is a fortiori responsible for the carrying out of obviously illegal and improper commands from superiors. As regards the so-called court-martial, the court cannot hold that it was a court-martial in any sense of the word. It was anything that the court pleases except a tribunal, martial or otherwise. It was a consultation, a conspiracy, a measure to mature a criminal purpose, but it was not a court. And even if it were, and even if the court were fully and properly constituted, still, according to the Manual of Military Law, the members of such court would be liable to be hanged if they had illegally carried out a sentence of death.

But these defences have really hardly been urged by the defence at all seriously. Counsel for the defence appears to rely mainly on the technical objection to the indictment raised first of all, on the nature of the warfare waged against the Bushveldt Carbineers, and on the fact that Visser was shot in retaliation for Captain Hunt's death. Now, the latter point is the strongest possible point in the case for the prosecution. It proves conclusively the malice of the prisoners. Captain Hunt, so far as they knew and had reason to suppose, was killed in fair fight, and there was even then nothing whatever to connect Visser with his death, and yet every one of the prisoners, as well as the counsel for the defence, admits that the real reason for shooting Visser was because Hunt had been killed. Could proof of malice conceivably be clearer? Counsel for the defence urges that retaliation is recognised as legitimate by the Manual of Military Law. That is a mere twisting of words, and I think it is hardly necessary for me to urge on a body of military men the danger of acknowledging the right of subaltern officers to avenge their private grievances on prisoners of war who happen to fall into their hands. Retaliation has a perfectly definite meaning in military law, and means the deliberate and authoritative taking of measures of reprisal, as answer to some action on the part of the enemy contrary to the customs of war, but it certainly does not mean that subordinate officers are entitled to shoot prisoners who fall into their hands because an officer of their regiment has been killed. There is not a grain of evidence to connect Visser with Hunt's death, nor to show that Hunt was not killed in fair fight.

As to Major Thomas' (counsel for defence) argument, based on the state of the country, could anything be more preposterous than to say that minor officers are entitled to make war on principles of barbarity approved only by themselves? If they do so they must abide by the consequences.

CHAPTER XV

CLOSE OF THE VISSER CASE

The Judge Advocate summed up as follows:--With reference to this case, it would appear that the prisoners considered that they had justification (in virtue of their instructions from the late Captain Hunt regarding the treatment of Boer prisoners of war) for the course they adopted, also that they acted under provocation and in ignorance.

The general rule is that a person is responsible for the natural consequences of his own acts. If several persons meet with a common intent to execute some criminal purpose, each is responsible for every offence committed by any one of them in furtherance of that purpose.

A person is in all cases fully responsible for any offence which is committed by another by his instigation, even though the offence may be committed in a different way from the one suggested. The fact that the blame is shared by another will not relieve a person contributing to the death from responsibility.

If a person has unlawfully caused death by conduct which was intended to cause death or grievous bodily harm to some person, whatever the intention of the offender may have been, he is guilty of murder. It may be taken generally that in all cases where a killing cannot be justified or excused, if it does not amount to murder it is manslaughter, and a person charged with murder can be convicted of manslaughter. Again, the offence is manslaughter if the act from which death results was committed under the influence of passion arising from extreme provocation; but it must be clearly established, in all cases where provocation is put forward as an excuse, that at the time when the crime was committed the offender was actually so completely under the influence of passion arising from the provocation that he was at that moment deprived of the power of self-control, and with this view it will be necessary to consider carefully the manner in which the crime was committed, the length of the interval between the provocation and the killing, the conduct of the offender during the interval, and all other circumstances tending to show his state of mind.

Ignorance of law is no defence to a criminal charge, but such ignorance may be properly taken into consideration in determining the amount of punishment to be awarded.

The essence of the crime of murder is malicious intent. I would point out that the prisoners did not carry out the order they allege to have received re the shooting of Boers in khaki until after the death of Captain Hunt, which they admit biassed their minds.

The rights of killing an armed man exists only so long as he resists; as soon as he submits he is entitled to be treated as a prisoner of war.

As regards the treatment of an enemy caught in the uniform of his opponent, it would have to be shown that he was wearing such uniform at the time with the deliberate intention of deceiving.

Enemies rendered harmless by wounds must not only be spared; but humanity commands that if they fall into the hands of their opponents the care taken of them should be second only to the care taken of the wounded belonging to the captors.

The prisoners, their escorts, and counsel then retired to the corridor while the court consulted upon a verdict; in a little over half an hour we were recalled. Glancing round the court, I noticed one of the members in tears. My attention was arrested, but I did not then attach any significance to it.

On our appearance in court we were requested to state our military service, which was as follows. Statement as to service by Lieutenant H. H. Morant, B.V.C.:--

"I have held a commission since 1st April, 1901, in the Bushveldt Carbineers.

"Prior to this I was in the South Australian Second Contingent for nine months. I was a sergeant in that corps, and was promoted to a commission out of that corps into the Transvaal Constabulary, but went home to England for six months. I came out again and joined the B.V.C.; since then I have been serving on detachment the whole time. I hand in a letter from the O.C. South Australians.

"In March, 1900, I was carrying despatches for the Flying Column to Prieska, under Colonel Lowe, 7th D.G. I was in the general advance to Bloemfontein, and took part in the engagements of 'Karee Siding and Kroonstadt and other engagements with Lord Roberts until the entry into Pretoria. I was at Diamond Hill, and then was attached to General French's staff, Cavalry Brigade, as war correspondent with Bennet Burleigh, for the London 'Daily Telegraph,' and accompanied that column through Belfast and Middleburg to the occupation of Barbeton, when I went home to England."

The letter from the O.C. South Australians read:--

My dear Morant,--There seems to be an immediate probability of the S.A. Regiment returning either to Australia or going to England, so I hasten to send you a line wishing you "Au Revoir." I desire to wish you most heartily every success in your future career, and to express my entire satisfaction with your conduct while with the South Australians. Your soldierly behaviour and your continual alertness as an irregular carried high commendation--and deservedly--from the whole of the officers of the regiment. I trust that in the future we may have an opportunity of renewing our pleasant acquaintanceship.

Statement by Lieutenant Picton:--

"I have been in South Africa two years on service. I hold my commission in the B.V.C. since last May. Previous to that I was attached to the 8th M.I., and served under Colonel Le Gallais. I have received the Distinguished Conduct Medal, and been mentioned in despatches. I have been three times wounded since the outbreak of the war.

"I produce three letters from different commanding officers under whom I have served, and could refer the court to Col. Hodgson, commanding 9th Area, Cape Colony.

"During the month I was in Spelonken under Capt. Hunt I took 37 prisoners, 50 rifles, 15 waggons, and 500 head of cattle, mules, horses, &c."

Letter (1) from Captain Savil, O.C. Loch's Horse:-- Sergeant Picton came out with Loch's Horse as a corporal in February, 1901. He has given entire satisfaction to his officers, and I am very pleased to state I have found him not only very plucky when in action, but steady and painstaking in the execution of his duty.

He has been recommended for the D.S.M. Having been under my personal command for some time, I cannot speak too highly of his good conduct.

Letter (2):-- This is to introduce to you Sergeant Picton, of my corps, Loch's Horse. He is a worthy fellow and well connected, and is seeking a commission. Could you help him in getting such, in your regiment? I understand you have some vacancies.

Letter (3) from Lieut.-Colonel Hickee, O.C. 8th M.I.:-- I am sending Sergeant Picton, Loch's Horse, for discharge. He has served with the 8th Corps M.I. for the last eleven months, and has been under my command since 9th November, 1900. I am able to say that he has carried out his duties in a most satisfactory manner.

He is a most efficient interpreter and a good man in the field, and was recommended to the C. in C. for his behaviour at Bothaville.

Statement by Lieutenant Handcock, B.V.C.:--

"I have served about twelve months in the New South Wales Mounted Infantry as a farrier; about two months in the Railway Police, Pretoria; and from the 22nd February last year in the Bushveldt Carbineers as veterinary lieutenant."

Statement by Lieutenant Witton, B.V.C.:--

"I have held a commission since June last in the B.V.C. I was previously in the 4th Contingent Imperial Bushmen (Victorian) as Q.M.S. for fourteen months. Formerly I was in the Victorian Permanent Artillery about twelve months as a gunner.

"I have also served nearly two years in the Victorian Rangers, Volunteer Corps.

"I received my commission for raising a gun detachment for the B.V.C."

CHAPTER XVI

THE EIGHT BOERS CASE

The Visser case was now over. Not the slightest hint was given that we had been found guilty, and a sentence passed; I was never informed as to the finding of the court regarding this case, but three years later I read in a newspaper summary of the evidence that I had been found guilty of manslaughter and cashiered. The case had barely concluded when Captain Burns-Begg, who had acted as prosecutor, was ordered to England. It seemed as though he was required at the War Office to give particulars personally of the trial and of the disclosures that had been made there. Major Bolton now took the place of Captain Burns-Begg; Major Ousely, D.S.O., and Captain Marshall were also relieved as members of the court, and their places were filled by Captains Matcham and Brown.

The reconstituted court started from Pretoria for Pietersburg on the 31st January.

When we entrained it was evident our social status had undergone a decided change. The accommodation provided was the same for the return trip as when going down, but this time we were not permitted to enter a carriage. After considerable delay a small, dirty, covered-in truck was attached to the train, into which we were crowded, with our escorts, servants, and baggage. It was a sweltering day in January, and the effect it had upon us is more easily imagined than described.

When nearing Warm Baths Station the train pulled up; it was reported that a party of Boers were crossing the line. A member of the court came to our little sheep-truck, and for the second time during our trial we were ordered to stand to arms. Morant prayed, as I am sure he never prayed in his life before, that we might get into action. The members of the court did not reciprocate his feelings, but did their best to avoid action, and kept the train at a standstill for over an hour while they carefully examined the surrounding country through their field-glasses, giving the Boers ample time to get out of sight. Then, moving on slowly from block-house to block-house, we safely passed the point of danger.

We arrived at Pietersburg on 1st February, and the court assembled again on the 3rd to adjudicate on what was called the eight Boers case. Morant, Handcock, and myself were arraigned on the charge of shooting or instigating others to shoot these. The main facts, as adduced by the evidence for the prosecution, were not disputed. At the close of the evidence for the prosecution, Major Thomas, the prisoners' counsel, made the following protest:--"I submit the charge of inciting to murder has not been proved. The prisoners are alleged to be accessories before the crime of murder. They are not charged with being conspirators, and I submit that the alleged charge of murder against the principals has not been established, and, if so, there can be no accessories. I submit that the proper way to have brought this case before the court should have been in the form of a charge for conspiracy."

The court ruled that the case must proceed. Major Thomas then said that he did not propose to put the prisoners in the box, as the main facts were not disputed, but statements would be handed in, and the evidence he would call would be confined to three things--orders received, the customs of the war, and the practices adopted in other irregular corps against the enemy when breaking the customs of war.

This is the statement made by Lieutenant H. H. Morant:--

"I do not feel called upon, nor am I advised by my counsel, that it is necessary for me to enter the witness-box in this case. In the case of Visser I gave the fullest explanation of my position and my instructions regarding the Boers captured in the Spelonken district. I was distinctly and repeatedly told by my late friend and commanding officer, Capt. Hunt, on our arrival at Spelonken, which happened a few days after the train-wrecking occurrence, that no Boer prisoners were in future to be taken. I have already shown in Visser's case, and can bring further evidence in this case, to prove that Capt. Hunt gave these orders not only to me, but to others under his command, that is, 'that no prisoners were to be taken,' and he reprimanded me for not carrying out this order.

"Capt. Hunt had been my most intimate friend in South Africa. We were engaged to two sisters in England. He joined the B.V.C. in order to be in the same regiment as myself, and he practically asked Major Lenehan that we might be together in the same squadron. Capt. Hunt had Imperial service in the 10th Hussars, and some colonial service in French's Scouts, and I had implicit confidence in him and regarded his orders as authoritative and bonb fide. Until Capt. Hunt's body was found stripped and mutilated I shot no prisoners, though I maintain it is generally known that Boers who had been concerned in misdoings and outrages, such as the nomadic Dutchmen of the Spelonken, had been executed summarily by many Irregular Corps who have done good work in South Africa. After Capt. Hunt's death and the brutal treatment of him, alive or dead, I resolved as his successor and survivor to carry out the orders he had impressed upon me, orders which other officers have in other places and in other corps carried out, with the provocation we had received. The Boers had left my friend's body, the body of an Englishman and officer, lying stripped, disfigured, and not buried--thrown into a drain like a pariah dog. Moreover, I had heard so much about the deeds of these particular Boers that I have charged with murder, reports which connect them with train wreckings and maraudings. I also know they belonged to the same gang that had maltreated and dishonoured the body of my friend and brother officer. I considered I was quite justified in not treating such men with the amenity usually accorded to prisoners of war, and I am quite satisfied that they fully deserved the summary execution they received. In ordering these Boers to be shot, I did so fully believing that, in view of what Capt. Hunt had so distinctly ordered me, and what I myself knew bad been done elsewhere, I was practically right and justified by the rules of guerilla warfare.

"I was Senior Officer of the B.V.C. in the Spelonken, and for the ordering of the shooting of these Boers I take full and entire responsibility. I admit having sent in an 'edited' report, but I did so for reasons which have actuated higher military authorities than myself. I have been told that I was never myself after the death of Capt. Hunt, and I admit that his death preyed upon my mind when I thought of the brutal treatment he had received. This treatment of Capt. Hunt's body, coupled with the train wreckings which had occurred, made me resolve to act on orders and do as other officers have done under less trying circumstances than myself.

"The alleged conversation between myself and Sergeant Wrench is absolutely untrue; No such conversation ever occurred. It is an entire fabrication."

Statement made by Lieutenant P. J. Handcock:--

"I am Veterinary Lieutenant. I have had a very poor education. I never cared much about being an officer; all I know is about horses, though I like to fight. Capt. Robinson said it was right to shoot traitors. Capt. Hunt told us when he came out that no Boers were to be taken. I had often heard that Boers were to be shot if they sniped or wore khaki or smashed up trains. I do not know what the rule under such things is, but we all thought that Capt. Hunt knew the correct thing. I did not much believe in Capt. Robinson, and when he ordered the man to be shot I told Capt. Hunt all about it. When he came to Spelonken, Capt. Hunt did not say it was wrong; he said we were not to take prisoners any more, so I thought he was doing his orders. I did what I was told to do, and I cannot say any more. No conversation ever took place between Sergeant Wrench and Lieutenant Morant in my presence, as stated by Sergeant Wrench in court."

Statement by Lieutenant Witton:--

"I had received my commission as a Lieutenant about six weeks before the 23rd August. I was told what the orders about Boers were as received from Captain Hunt, and I took it they were correct; I did whatever I was told, and raised no question one way or the other, as it is customary to obey orders.

"Capt. Hunt and Lieut. Morant were great friends, and I supposed that all orders were correct that Capt. Hunt gave. He was greatly relied upon by all when he came to reform matters at Spelonken, after Captain Robinson left.

"On the 23rd August one of the Boers rushed at me to seize my carbine, and I shot at him to keep him off."

Lieutenant Picton gave evidence that he was moving out with a patrol towards Scinde, when Captain Hunt gave him instructions not to bring back any prisoners. He got some prisoners on this patrol and brought them back to Fort Edward, and was reprimanded for doing so. One of the prisoners was a man named Venter. He was sent to the Burgher Camp, and was one of those who escaped from there and went on commando with Beyers. "He was shot during the attack on Pietersburg, and I recognised him."

Captain Taylor was called to give evidence for the defence, and stated that he remembered one time when Lieutenant Morant brought in prisoners; he was asked by Captain Hunt why he brought them in; Capt. Hunt said they should have been shot.

This witness was cross-examined by the Prosecutor as follows:--"Were you not Officer Commanding of the Spelonken ?" He replied: "Yes; of the district."

The exact words used by Captain Hunt when reprimanding Morant were tersely related by another witness:--"What the hell do you mean by bringing these men in? We have neither room nor rations for them here."

Numerous witnesses were called to prove that Captain Hunt had given distinct orders that no prisoners were to be taken, and others to prove what had been done to their knowledge in other corps. The Judge Advocate twice protested that the evidence that was being produced was extremely irrelevant, and the rule was that nothing should be admitted as evidence that did not tend immediately to prove or disprove the charge in criminal proceedings.

One witness, an Intelligence Agent, gave evidence that he had seen a Boer summarily dealt with, who had been captured fully dressed in khaki.

Another witness gave evidence that in his column it was published in orders that Boers captured wearing khaki were to be summarily dealt with.

Cable messages also appeared in the Australian press, dated November, 1901, that Lord Kitchener had issued orders that all Boers who were captured wearing the khaki uniform of British troops should be shot.

It was also stated in another cablegram received a short time before this that a number of Boers wearing khaki belonging to the commando of Commandant Smutz had been captured by Colonel Gorringe, and had been shot.

The ordinary regulations provide that in time of peace any person found wearing a military uniform of the British forces, when not entitled to do so, may be fined #10, while for the same offence in time of war the death penalty can be exacted.

In the face of this Major Bolton went into the witness-box, where he said that he had "no knowledge" of a proclamation that Boers taken in khaki were to be shot.

This was the time Lord Kitchener should have been put in the box, and the facts of the case and all necessary information obtained direct from him in the interests of justice and the Empire generally.

(This incident came under my notice while we were being tried at Pietersburg. A small patrol of the Pietersburg Light Horse, mostly raw recruits, went out scouting. When approaching a farm house they saw several men walking about dressed in a similar fashion to themselves; they rode up, dismounted, and entered into conversation. They were greatly astonished when they were covered by the rifles of the others, and ordered to hand over their arms and ammunition. Upon this being done, they were requested to hand over their uniforms; when they were stripped they were allowed to return in a nude state to Pietersburg. The party into whose hands they had fallen were a party of Irish-Americans fighting with the Boers.)

Major R. W. Lenehan, late of the Bushveldt Carbineers, gave evidence that Lieutenant Handcock was a veterinary officer, and that he had not wished him to go to Spelonken, but upon representation being made he allowed him to go. Mr. Handcock had a very strong sense of duty, and anything he was ordered to do he would do without the slightest question, no matter what it might be.

Major Thomas, the prisoners' counsel, then handed in his address, as follows, which was read and attached to proceedings:--

The main facts, as adduced by the evidence for the prosecution, are not denied by the defence. The long statement, alleged to have been made by Lieutenant Morant to the witness Wrench is denied, and the court must form its own opinion, from the attitude of Wrench, as to whether or not he has not drawn considerably upon a rather vindictive imagination for his glibly-told story. But even if true, this does not affect the real issue. Apart from any question of law, such as was raised at the conclusion of the evidence for the prosecution, and which this court perhaps can scarcely deal with, the prisoners' defence is that, no matter in what way the charge against them has been, or might have been framed, the action they respectively took in the summary execution of these eight Boers was justifiable, or, at any rate, not criminal. That which would be a crime, a felony, or a malicious act in time of peace may be quite justifiable in time of war, and doubly so in guerilla warfare, waged against men who cannot be regarded as lawful belligerents, but only as lawless bands of marauders, who carry on desultory hostilities, combined with train wreckings and other uncivilised practices. Upon such an enemy I maintain our troops are justified in making the severest reprisals, and are entitled to regard them, not as lawful belligerents at all, but as outlaws.

But having regard to the immensely wide area over which the present war in South Africa has for more than two years extended, the nature of the country, and the peculiar class of people who keep the fighting going, it happens that, whilst in one part of the theatre of war the enemy's methods may be such that we cannot take great exception to them, how ever senseless and infatuated the prolongation of the strife may seem to us, yet in other parts of the country quite a different kind of operations are in vogue, operations of such a nature that they must be treated as uncivilised and often barbarous. In one district we

93

may meet a large organised body of Boers fighting under a recognised and honourable commandant, whilst in another district we find ourselves pitted against roving bands under no recognised leader. It was against the latter class, and especially during the months of July, August, and September last, that the small Spelonken detachment of the Bushveldt Carbineers, to which the prisoners belonged, were sent out to operate under special orders. A small body, about 100 strong, they had to work over a vast area of difficult country, where, in small patrols and parties they had literally to hunt down the shifting bands of the enemy, in kloofs and almost inaccessible places, taking their lives in their hands. And sufficient evidence has come out during these cases to show how excellently their work was done. Practically they cleared the Spelonken district of Boers, many of whom found harbour there after their exploits against trains on the Pietersburg line. Even the prosecution admit that these Boers were of a bad class, and that this was the character of some, if not of all, of the eight men alleged to have been murdered.

We have shown that train wreckers were in the district at this particular period, and we have put in an official return of their doings in this respect, starting from 4th July last. On that date a train-wrecking occurred, in which an officer and a number of men were killed--the officer being a friend of the late Captain Hunt. Closely following upon this, Captain Hunt was sent to take charge of the Spelonken detachment, and it is abundantly proved that his orders were "No prisoners" after this-no quarter. He impressed this upon his officers and non-commissioned officers, and reprimanded them for non-observance of his orders. He had been in the regular army, and his instructions, coming as he did to institute a new order of things at Spelonken, were entitled to weight from irregular subordinates. It was quite evident that they were guided by him, but it was not until Hunt himself was killed, with rather brutal surrounding circumstances, that his directions were fulfilled. After this his successor, Lieutenant Morant, as he says, resolved to carry out previous orders. Up to this Morant had been particularly lenient towards prisoners, and there is no proof (but the very opposite) of his being of a malicious or cruel nature. It is true that after Hunt's death he changed a good deal, and adopted the sternest measures against the enemy. In civil life, and if trying a civil offence, under civil and peaceful conditions, it might be said that he became revengeful, but in time of war revenge and retaliation are allowable. It would be cant and hypocrisy to maintain otherwise. War makes men's natures both callous and, on occasions, revengeful. What is the object of war? Simply to kill and disable as many men of the opposite side as possible. In pursuing these objects, soldiers are not to be judged by the rules of citizen life, and often, as soldiers, they do things, which, calmly regarded afterwards or in time of peace, appear, and are, unchristian and even brutal.

The more civilised the foe we deal with the more chivalric the methods of warfare, and the brutal element is absent or rarely apparent. But when the civilised rules and customs of war are departed from by one side, reprisals follow from the other, and then the bad, the bitter, the revengeful side of war is seen. If in every war, especially guerilla war, officers and men who committed reprisals were to be brought up and tried as murderers, court-martials might be kept going all the year. Such might be the case in the present war, if all the reprisals, summary executions, slaughters, were dragged before formal courts, argued over by counsel and prosecutor as to points of law, and all the gruesome details exposed to the light of day.

We cannot judge such matters fairly unless we place ourselves amidst the same surroundings, and with the same provocations as obtained with the men whose actions are to be tried. What are our irregular troops for? To ride down, harry, and shoot the enemy, and I submit, if the latter deserve it, to adopt strong retaliatory measures. These irregular combatants of the army are really charged now with the bulk of the fighting, and if they are to be restrained and tied down by strict rules, such as might obtain were they fighting French or German soldiers instead of guerillas, then the sooner they are recalled from the field the better, or, at any rate, let definite instructions be issued for their guidance. Do not let them have indefinite, hazy instructions as to what they may do. Do not let us have officers reprimanded by their seniors for hampering the column with prisoners, and at another time, and another place, haul them up as murderers because they do the opposite. I fear there is a great deal of rather mawkish sentimentality about some of these Boer bands, who do so much to keep this prolonged war going in spite of the marvellously good treatment the British have extended towards their people, wives and children.

I refer again to the class of Boers which had to be combated in the Spelonken in July, August, and September, and I maintain that it was to be presumed, and the actions of other irregular corps elsewhere show, that the Bushveldt Carbineers were not singular in this respect, that if the foe committed outrages, and departed from the customs of war, punitive measures might be adopted. If these officers have over-stepped the mark they should be upheld. The Boers brought these measures on themselves, and should take the consequences of their collective acts in the district. We cannot discriminate as to who did this or that; they must all be regarded as involved in, or countenancing nefarious practices which provoked reprisal. Their own countrymen are beginning to become disgusted with the prevailing methods, and in hundreds are joining the British, in hope of stopping the useless fighting which is desolating their country, and keeping all South Africa chafing under martial law. South Africa is a cosmopolitan country, and what affects the British affects large numbers of Germans and other foreigners, who are excluded from their homes or from settling here. For the interests of the foreigner, and even the Dutch themselves, as well as the British our troops are fighting, and on our irregulars falls the brunt of it. Are we to recognise them as, irregulars or as regulars? From irregulars irregularities are to be expected, and cannot be avoided. Let us, if we employ them in guerilla tactics, either definitely instruct them by clear orders and proclamations as to how far they may go, or uphold them if they have not been so instructed and thus fallen into error. If these arguments apply in ordinary cases, they have especial force in the present case, where Lieut. Morant acted under express directions conveyed to him by his deceased superior officer, and if he followed these instructions when he himself took over command, believing that he was justified in following them, then any "criminal intent" is disproved, and if this applies to Lieut. Morant, it applies again with still greater force to his subordinate lieutenants, Handcock and Witton. Lieut. Morant honourably acknowledges in his written statement the responsibilities of his position as senior officer, but that he also takes upon himself the burden of a crime is repudiated and denied.

In conclusion, I would quote the following passages from the Chapter on Customs of War, as comprised in the Manual of Military Law, issued for our guidance by the Army, remembering, however, that no precise rules can be laid down to meet all the varying styles of warfare. Such rules can be but guides as to our actions, and in default of clear orders abrogating these, I submit that they are to be followed as far as applicable.

"The first duty of a citizen is to defend his country, but this defence must be conducted according to the Customs of War." Further, "War must be conducted by persons acting under the control of some recognised Government, having power to put an end to hostilities, in order that the enemy may know the authority to which he may resort when desirous of making peace." Under ordinary circumstances, therefore, persons committing acts of hostility who do not belong to an organised body, authorised by some recognised Government, and do not wear a military uniform, or some conspicuous dress or mark, showing them to be part of an organised military body, incur the risk of being treated as marauders and punished accordingly.

"Persons, other than regular troops in uniform, whose dress shows their character, committing acts of hostility against an enemy, must, if they expect when captured to be treated as prisoners of war, be organised in such a manner, or fight under such circumstances, as to give their opponents due notice that they are open enemies from whom resistance is to be expected."

"Retaliation is military vengeance; it takes place where an outrage committed on one side is avenged by the commission of a similar act on the other."

CHAPTER XVII

THE SECOND COURT-MARTIAL (Continued)

As reference was made by Major Thomas to a witness named Wrench, I attach his evidence:--

On the 19th August you were sent out to take charge of some prisoners?

On the 19th August I went out with nine men to bring in some prisoners. The prisoners were handed to me by Ledeboer, of the Intelligence. Five bolts were also given to me, taken out of the prisoners' rifles, and these were distributed amongst the men. We returned, and arrived at the hospital on the evening of the 22nd August, and camped there for the night. On the morning of the 23rd August, at about 7 a.m., Lieuts. Morant, Handcock, and Witton, Sergt.-Major Hammett, and Troopers Duckett and Thompson, came out. Mr. Morant informed me that Tom Kelly, with about forty Boers, were in the immediate vicinity. Mr. Morant gave me orders to saddle up and inspan the waggon at once, and get on the road. I was to extend the men well away in the bush, and keep in the centre of the road myself, and to skirmish at least a mile ahead of the waggon.

Mr. Morant said I was to keep a sharp look-out, as no doubt I would hear firing, and when I did so I was to immediately gallop back to him. When we first came in sight of Bristow's Farm, one shot was fired by somebody hidden. I then gave orders to dismount, and then two other shots were heard in the same place, the farm. I did not go back to report this to Mr. Morant. Shortly afterwards about fifteen shots, as far as we could make out, were fired in our rear, at least 1000 yards behind. I then gave the order to mount, and we went on to Bristow's Farm, to report to Captain Taylor, having received instructions to do so from Mr. Morant. I reported the arrival of the patrol to Capt. Taylor, who was walking about in front of the house in a very excited state. I told Capt. Taylor I had handed over the eight Boers to Mr. Morant and his party. Some time after this I was sent for by Mr. Morant. Mr. Morant and Mr. Handcock were lying each in their beds. Mr. Morant had a letter in his hand, and said to me that I had made a fool of myself, and that this was the letter reporting me, and that it would very likely mean a court-martial for me. After a little conversation Mr. Morant said "Don't let us beat about the bush. From what I can see of it, there are several men here who don't agree with this shooting. I want you to go round to the men and find out those who are willing to do it and those who are not, and then we will soon get rid of those who don't agree. I had orders to weed out the Fort, which you know I did, but I still find there are a lot of sentimental left. I have had several letters of congratulation from headquarters over the last fight, and now I've started I mean to go on with it. From what I can see of it, you had a rotten lot of men, but we will give you another chance. I shall send out a small patrol in a few days; I shall pick my own men this time, and send you with them." When Mr. Morant spoke of finding the men who were agreeable and who were not, Lieut. Handcock said, if he could only get ten men, that would be sufficient for his purpose.

Did Mr. Morant say why you were to be tried by court-martial?

Yes. That three parties of our people met the Boer prisoners returning to the Fort, who were not guarded, which was not true. He said the first party were Kaffir scouts. I said that that did not amount to much. The next party were our own Intelligence. I then asked who the third party were. He said, "Don't let us beat about the bush," and then the subject started.

Do you know who fired the three shots that were heard?

No. They were fired from the farm.

Wrench was cross-examined by the Counsel for the Prisoners.

This conversation you refer to, is it related exactly as it occurred?

Not exactly, but words to that effect. I have not added to it. I may have left something out. It occurred about 8 o'clock. I was not in bed. We were playing cards. The two officers were in bed when this conversation took place. It occurred about a week after the Boers were shot--about the 30th August.

You once got yourself into trouble in the Spelonken with Captain Hunt?

No, never.

Is it not a fact that you were reported for insolent conduct to Sergt.-Major Clark, and were reprimanded for it?

I did not get on well with Sergt.-Major Clark.

On account of your bad conduct, were you not threatened to be tied up to a waggon by Captain Hunt?

No, never.

Did you not ask Mr. Morant to save you from that taking place?

No, but I spoke to Mr. Morant, and reported the conduct of Sergt.-Major Clark on patrol to Saltpan.

Was anyone else present except Mr. Morant and Mr. Handcock?

No; only those two.

Wrench was examined by the court:--

"How many prisoners did you hand over?"

"Eight. They were voluntary surrenders."

"Were you present when they surrendered?"

"No. I was not present when they surrendered."

"Then you do not know whether they were captured prisoners or had voluntarily surrendered?"

"Ledeboer said they had surrendered to him."

A statement of the trains wrecked in the district from 4th July, 1901, was also put in:--

The first wreck occurred on 4th July, about five miles north of Naboonspruit. There were killed and died of wounds: One officer (Lieut. Best, Gordon Highlanders) and fifteen men, three natives. Wounded: Seven Gordon Highlanders, one native.

The second attempt at train-wrecking occurred on 10th August, 1901, 3 1/2 miles N. if Groon Vlei (about 12 or 13 miles N. of Nylstroom). Lieut. Burnett, Gordon Righlanders, beat off Boers. No record of our casualties, which were very slight.

The third train wreck occurred on 3ist August, 1901, at Kilo 35, between Waterfall and Haman's Kraal. Killed and died of wounds: One officer (Col. Vandeleur), twelve men, and two natives. Wounded: Twenty officers and men.

The Prosecution handed in a written reply as follows:--

I submit to the court that the witnesses have shown by their evidence, which is very clear, that on the evening of the 22nd August the prisoners Lieut. Morant and Lieut. Handcock sent for Troopers Thompson and Duckett and warned them for a patrol the following morning, telling them at the time that they were going out to shoot eight Boer prisoners or surrenders.

About 5 a.m., 23rd August, the patrol, consisting of Lieuts. Morant, Handcock, Witton, Sergeant-Major Hammett, and Troopers Duckett and Thompson, left Fort Edward and proceeded towards Elim Hospital, where they met Sergeant Wrench in charge of the eight Boers. Lieut. Morant told the members of this patrol that these men were to be shot, and that the signal for this would be when he said, "have you any more information," or some words to that effect. Sergt. Wrench was ordered to proceed then with his patrol to the Fort, Lieut. Morant taking charge of the prisoners with his party. About half way back the convoy halted, and the eight men, who were unarmed, were ordered about twenty paces off the road and questioned by Lieut. Morant, and on his giving the signal were shot down by the members of this patrol. The defence do not in any way question these facts materially, but try to justify them in three ways:--

Firstly: That they were only carrying out orders from superior authority. All I have to say on this head is that such orders, if given, do not constitute a lawful command and need not be obeyed.

Secondly: That other irregular corps had done the same thing. Even if so, two wrongs do not make a right.

Lastly: That the character of these men was such that they did not deserve any other treatment. I must submit to the court that, even if these men had been caught red-handed committing some outrage, they, once having surrendered or been taken prisoners and disarmed, were entitled to our protection until such time as they would be brought to trial.

I have nothing further to say, and so leave it to the court to say if the prisoners are guilty of the crime of which they are charged, or if their acts were such as are customary in civilised warfare.

CHAPTER XVIII

IN THE NAME OF JUSTICE!

The following is the summing-up by the Judge Advocate

In the case now under consideration the prisoners practically admit having committed the offence with which they stand charged, but maintain that they had justification for the course they pursued, and that there was palliation for their action owing to the fact, as alleged by them, that similar occurrences have taken place during the course of this war, and have been ignored or condoned.

I would point out that two wrongs do not make a right, and that the commission of a wrongful act can scarcely be urged as a justification for the repetition of that act.

I would point out that war is not a relation of man to man, but of State to State, and of itself implies no private hostility between the individuals by whom it is carried on.

The object of war is the redress by force of a national injury. Wars are the highest trials of right, and it is scarcely seemly that they should degenerate into a medium of personal revenge. Retaliation is military vengeance. It takes place when an outrage committed on one side is avenged by the commission of a similar act on the other.

Retaliation is the extreme right of war, and should be resorted to only in the last necessity, and then only by someone in authority. The first principle of war is that armed forces, so long as they resist, may be destroyed by all legitimate means.

The right of killing an armed man exists only so long as he resists; as soon as he submits he is entitled to be treated as a prisoner of war. Quarter should never be refused to men who surrender, unless they have been guilty of some such violation of the customs of war as would of itself expose them to the penalty of death, and even when so guilty they should be put on their trial before being executed, as it is seldom justifiable for a combatant to take the law into his own hands against an unresisting foe.

Where an act complained of is itself unlawful, bona fides or honesty of purpose is no excuse; how far a subordinate could plead the specific commands of a superior, such commands being not obviously improper or contrary to law, as justifying an injury inflicted, is doubtful.

The rule is that a person is responsible for the natural consequence of his acts.

If several persons go out with a common intent to execute some criminal purpose, each is responsible for every offence committed by any one of them in furtherance of that purpose. A person is in all cases fully responsible for any offence which is committed by another by his instigation.

If a person has unlawfully caused death by conduct which was intended to cause death or grievous bodily harm to some person, whatever the intention of the offender may have been, he is guilty of murder. If a person is proved to have killed another, the law presumes prima facie that he is guilty of murder.

It will be on the accused to prove such facts as may reduce the offence to manslaughter, or excuse him from all criminal responsibility. It may be taken generally that in all cases where a killing cannot be justified, if it is not murder it is manslaughter; again, the offence is manslaughter if the act from which death results was committed under the influence of passion arising from extreme provocation, but it must be clearly established in cases when provocation is put forward as an excuse that at the time the crime was committed the offender was so completely under the influence of passion arising from the provocation that he was at that moment deprived of the power of self-control, and with this view it will be necessary to consider carefully--(1) The manner in which the crime was committed, whether deliberately and with premeditation, and also (2) the length of the interval between the provocation and the killing, so as to establish the fact that the alleged provocation was a justification of the crime.

I must further draw the attention of the court to the fact that much irrelevant evidence has been allowed to be produced, which will require careful sifting before they can arrive at a just finding.

The conclusion of this case was similar to the first, our military service being again taken. No intimation was given as to the nature of the verdict or the sentence.

This concluded the charges against me, and I was not required to attend subsequent sittings of the court; my guard was now more relaxed than hitherto. Often I went about the garrison unattended, and in the company of an unarmed non-commissioned officer frequently visited friends in the town.

On the afternoon following the conclusion of the "eight Boers" case I attended a cricket match, which took place on the town cricket-ground, mingling with, among others, the president and members of the court, who had only the previous day, though I was not then aware of it, passed upon me the extreme penalty of the law, "To suffer death by being shot." With the exception of a surprised kind of stare from the haughty president, my presence there was unheeded. Incidents such as these tended to convince me that the penalty hanging over me could not be a very serious one. We were often provided with horses, and permitted to take riding exercise in the morning before breakfast.

The trial of Major Lenehan was now proceeded with. The charge against him was that, being on active service, he culpably neglected his duty by failing to report the shooting by men of his regiment, the Bushveldt Carbineers, of two men and a "boy." He pleaded "Not guilty." The main evidence in this case was given by Trooper Botha, a Dutchman, who had been Lieutenant Morant's favourite servant, though he was proved to have been at heart a traitor, for as soon as Morant got into trouble he immediately turned round and did him every harm in his power. There are men who could testify to hearing Botha ask Morant's permission to shoot Visser; he was allowed as a volunteer to form one of the firing party that did shoot him, yet at the court-martial he stated in evidence that he had objected to form one of the firing party, which was absolutely untrue.

Some time after the conclusion of the trials Trooper Botha was "accidentally" shot. His death could not be attributed to the condemned officers, as two had taken their departure to another world, the rest for other lands.

This Botha stated "that the three Boers were being brought in by Captain Taylor's Police, and were shot by five of the Carbineers; he reported what had been done to Morant in the presence of Major Lenehan." The five Carbineers of the patrol were Lieutenants Morant and Handcock, Sergeant-Major Hammett, Corporal McMahon, and Trooper Botha.

Major Lenehan had arrived at Fort Edward on the very day that these three men were shot. I had met him going out as I was on my way to Pietersburg with prisoners. During dinner, at which were present Major Lenehan, Captain Taylor, Lieutenants Morant and Handcock, and Surgeon Leonard, an argument arose regarding the trustworthiness of Dutchmen on British service. Captain Taylor said they were not trustworthy, but Morant maintained the affirmative. In support of his arguments he sent for Botha, and in reply to questions put by Morant, he said he was a good soldier, and had done his duty and shot Boers.

Major Lenehan was further charged with having failed to report that a trooper of the Carbineers, Van Buren, had been shot by Lieutenant Handcock. He pleaded "Not guilty." Ex-Captain Robertson was the principal witness for the prosecution in this case. He said he knew Van Buren, who had been shot; he had been warned that he was not to be trusted, and men refused to go on duty with him. He, Taylor, arid Handcock had a talk over it, and decided he was to be shot. He said that he made a report of this occurrence, and also of the shooting of six men, to Major Lenehan. The report made of Van Buren's death was not a true one; he had concealed the true facts in the interests of the corps.

Major Lenehan, in his defence, said that he had never been informed of the actual manner of Van Buren's death.

The counsel for the defence, Major Thomas, referred to the fact that Major Lenehan had already been, under arrest for three months (similar to that of the other officers), and protested against an officer being kept so long without trial. Robertson was the man who should have reported, and he had done so falsely. He and Taylor were the men who should have been prosecuted, but Robertson had been allowed to resign unconditionally. The verdict and the sentence were not made known.

The next case was then gone on with. Lieutenants Morant and Handcock were charged with instigating the killing of two men and one boy, names unknown.

Sergeant-Major Hammett deposed that he formed one of the patrol which the prisoners accompanied in search of three Boers. It was agreed that when the Boers were discovered, and Morant asked, "Do you know Captain Hunt" they were to be shot. This was done.

In this case Lieutenant Morant again chose to go into the witness-box, and gave evidence on oath. He deposed that he went out to look for the three Dutchmen. He never asked them to surrender; they were Dutchmen with whom we were at war, and belonged to a party which had stripped and mutilated a brother officer, and he had them shot.

Major Bolton was asked if he wished to cross-examine the witness, and upon replying in the affirmative Morant sprang up, and passionately exclaimed, "Look here, Major, you are just the 'Johnnie' I have been waiting to be cross-examined by; cross-examine me as much as you like, but let us have a straight gallop." In the cross-examination Morant's retorts were so straight and so bitter that they resulted in the collapse of the Prosecutor after a very few questions had been asked.

The court then sat to hear the charges against Captain Alfred Taylor, who was accused of murder in inciting Sergeant-Major Morison, Sergeant Oldham, and others to kill and murder six men, names unknown.

The following is a summary of the evidence taken:--

Sergeant-Major Morison, Bushveldt Carbineers, deposed that on 2nd July preceding he paraded his patrol and reported to Captain Robertson. The accused was present, and said he had intelligence that six Boers with two waggons were coming in to surrender, but that he would have no prisoners. The witness asked Captain Robertson if he should take orders from Taylor. Captain Robertson said, "Certainly, as he is commanding officer at Spelonken." Morison asked Taylor to repeat his order, which he did, saying that if the Boers showed the white flag the witness was not to see it. The witness repeated these orders to Sergeant Oldham, and warned six men and a corporal to accompany Oldham as an advance party. Six Boers were shot by the advance guard. These were the only ones met with that day. The patrol went on, and the following day a larger party of Boers with women and children was brought in, Taylor and Picton going to meet them.

Sergeant Oldham stated that the previous witness warned him of six Boers, and told him he was to make them fight, and on no account bring them in alive. The Boers were ambushed. There was a man in front of a waggon holding a white flag, and a great noise in the waggon. Oldham stopped the fire, thinking there might be women and children, but since he found only six men, as described in the orders, they were taken out and shot. He believed the flag was put up after the firing commenced. The Boers were armed and their rifles loaded. A good many prisoners were afterwards taken and sent into Pietersburg. The witness addressed his report of the affair to Captain Taylor by Morison's orders. Captain Robertson complained, and the report was readdressed to him. Neither Taylor nor Robertson were present at the shooting of the Boers.

Trooper Heath corroborated this. He said the Boers were dis-armed, lined out on the road, and shot.

Ex-Captain Robertson corroborated, and said that he had told Morison he must take his orders from the accused. Oldham reported, "All correct; they are all shot," and the witness saw the bodies.

Cross-examined, the witness admitted having had to resign and having been refused admission to any other corps. Morison re-ported that he was threatened with arrest. Morison demanded an inquiry, but broke his arrest and went to Pietersburg. Taylor asked for the patrol, as six armed Boers with two waggons were reported. Mori-son did not receive instructions from Taylor in the witness's presence. It was usual for patrols to get orders from Taylor.

Major Lenehan deposed to receiving orders to supply fifty of-ficers and men to proceed to Spelonken with Taylor. An inquiry was held in regard to charges in which Robertson and Morison were mixed up. Colonel Hall decided that it was better that Morison should go. This closed the case for the prosecution.

The accused elected to give evidence in his own defence. He said that during July last year he was in charge of natives and intelli-gence work. He was formerly a lieutenant in Plumer's Scouts, and came down on special service. No part of his instructions authorised him not to take prisoners. He had no military command. His instruc-tions went to the officer commanding the detachment of Bushveldt Carbineers. Colonel Hall's instructions were that a detachment of sixty men were to assist him in the Zoutpansberg. He gave instructions to the officers, telling the number of men required for patrols if any Boers had to be fought or captured. He never in-interfered with non-commissioned officers but once, when Lieutenant Picton placed Mori-son under arrest, and the witness refused the latter permission to go to Pietersburg, although he nevertheless broke his arrest and went. The witness received intelligence of certain Boers coming in to surrender, but never of the party of six. He never gave Morison any orders, and knew nothing about the six Boers, nor had he asked for a patrol to meet them. That patrol took three days' rations with it. The patrol af-terwards brought in parties of Boers of which the witness had been advised. The first intimation he had received of the charge of six Boers having been shot was made yesterday in court.

Davidson, clerk to the accused, deposed to the fact that letters addressed to the latter giving intelligence of the Boers were missing from the office after someone else took the witness' place. The empty file was found at his successor's office.

Otto Schwatz, an intelligence agent, spoke to having reported to Taylor the intention of two parties of Boers to surrender, but said he had never mentioned a party of six. Taylor was angry about the shooting of these Boers.

Further evidence for the defence was taken to show animus on the part of Morison.

Counsel addressed the court, who deliberated, and found the prisoner "Not guilty."

CHAPTER XIX

THE GERMAN MISSIONARY CASE

The trial of the last, and what was considered the most important case, that of the murder of the alleged German missionary, was opened on the 17th February. Lieutenant Handcock was charged with having killed Mr. Hess; Lieutenant Morant was charged with the offence of inciting to murder. For some unknown reason this case was heard privately in the garrison, and not publicly in the town, as the others had been.

Another court was also constituted, with Lieutenant Colonel McVean, C.B., Gordon Highlanders, as president. The members were:----Major L. L. Nichol, Rifle Brigade; Major E. Brereton, Northampton Regiment; Captain E. Comerwell, York Regiment; Captain Stapylton, Royal Field Artillery; Captain Rhodes, Welsh Regiment; and Captain Kent, Northampton Regiment.

Morant and Handcock pleaded "Not guilty," and the following evidence was adduced:--

Trooper Phillip deposed that on 23rd August preceding he was on Cossack Post duty, when a Cape cart, containing the missionary and a Cape boy, was going in the direction of Pietersburg. The missionary showed a pass signed by Capt. Taylor. He was greatly agitated, saying there had been a fight that morning and several had been killed, but he did not say whether they were British or Boers.

Corporal Sharp said that he had seen Morant addressing Hesse, and had afterwards seen Handcock riding in the same direction as the missionary. It was about 10 or 11 a.m. when the missionary went past, and Handcock went about 12. The latter had a carbine. He did not take the same road as the missionary.

Cross-examined, the witness admitted that he had gone a long way to fetch one Van Rooyen, who, he thought, was an eye-witness of the killing of the missionary. He did tell Trooper Hodd that he would walk barefooted from Spelonken to Pietersburg to be of the firing party to shoot Morant. He admitted that Handcock had issued an order against soldiers selling their uniforms, in consequence of the witness having done so. He had made it his business to collect notes of what was going on at Spelonken.

Two witnesses said that Handcock had left the fort that day with a rifle. He was on a chestnut horse. It was not unusual for an officer to carry a rifle.

A native deposed to having seen an armed man on horseback following the missionary. The man was on a brown horse. The witness afterwards heard shots, and then saw the dead body of a coloured boy. He took fright and fled. This was about 2 p.m. Trooper Thompson testified to having seen the missionary speaking to the Boers who were shot.

Other witnesses gave evidence as to having seen Hesse speak to Taylor while Morant was present after the shooting of eight men.

H. van Rooyen gave evidence as to having spoken to the Rev. Hesse on the road about 2 p.m. The witness trekked on with his waggon till sundown, when he saw a man on horseback coming from the direction of Pietersburg. The man turned off the road. Afterwards the man came on foot to the witness. He could not say if it was the same man that he had seen on horseback. The man on foot was Handcock, who advised the witness to push on, as Boers were about.

Trooper Botha deposed that he was one of the patrol of which Handcock had charge, and which found the missionary's body.

The case for the presecution then closed.

The accused Morant deposed that on 23rd August eight Boers guilty of train-wrecking and other crimes were shot by his orders. Hesse spoke to these Boers, and was told not to do so. Afterwards the witness saw Hesse in a cart. He produced a pass signed by Taylor. The witness advised him not to go on to Pietersburg because of the Boers. Hesse said he would chance it, and by the witness' advice he tied a white flag to the cart. The prisoner returned to the fort and then went to Taylor's, and he afterwards saw Handcock at Bristow's. Handcock went on to Schiels'. The prisoner never made any suggestion about killing the missionary. He was on good terms with him.

The accused Handcock made a statement as to his doings on that day. He said he left on foot for Schiels' in the morning, taking the road which branched off to the Pietersburg-road, and then across country. He lunched at Schiels', and then went to Bristow's till dusk, then back to the fort.

Mrs. Schiels, who lived on a farm about three miles from Fort Edward, the wife of Colonel Schiels, an artillery officer, who had fought with the Boers, and had been captured and sent as a prisoner to St. Helena, gave evidence that Lieutenant Handcock had lunch at her house on the 23rd August, and left during the afternoon.

Mrs. Bristow, who lived about a mile from Fort Edward, and was not on speaking terms with Mrs. Schiels, was the wife of an old settler in the district who had not taken any part in the war. This witness deposed that Lieutenant Handcock had been at their place on the afternoon of the 23rd August, and had returned to the fort in the evening.

The court gave a verdict of "Not guilty" in the case of both prisoners.

CHAPTER XX

EXECUTION OF MORANT AND HANDCOCK

After the conclusion of the trials, we waited three days to hear our fate; at times Morant appeared much worried, and gloomy forebodings would sometimes depress him. He would often say to me: "What do you think they will do with us? Do you think they will shoot us?"

On one of these days I was spending the afternoon with Morant, Handcock, and Picton at the prison. We whiled away the time in the garden at the back, where grew several peach trees laden with green fruit. When anyone passed with whom we were intimately acquainted, he would be saluted with a shower of hard peaches. Presently there came along in an old ricketty buggy a deposed Kaffir chief, Magato, who was in the employ of the Intelligence Department as a spy, and who had just before tried to swindle Morant out of a kaross, or rug of skins; he was greeted with a volley of the hard fruit. Appearing to take no notice, he drove straight away, and lodged a complaint with the Garrison Adjutant. Half an hour later Major Lenehan received an official letter from the Adjutant to the effect that complaints had been made about the conduct of his officers at the garrison prison, and requesting that he should cause the same to be discontinued.

The correspondence was passed on to Lieutenant Morant, and on the back of it he dashed off this reply:--

EXECUTION OF MORANT AND HANDCOCK

An Intelligence Nigger named Magato Has been singing a sad obligato, And begs to complain He suffered much pain By being struck with a squashy tomato. [P.S.--For "tomato" read "peach"-- exigency of verse.]

This was returned to the Adjutant; that night at dinner, in the officers' mess, it was handed round the table, to the great amusement of all.

On the night of the 20th the last remnant of the Carbineers met at a dinner at Morant's quarters in the garrison prison. Majors Thomas and Lenehan, Captain Taylor, Lieutenants Morant, Handcock, Picton and myself were there. The evening passed very pleasantly; the wearisome trials were forgotten, and it seemed like old times again. As if to fill our cup of joy to the very brim, an orderly from the brigade office came and informed Morant that a staff-officer had said in his hearing that the result of the court-martial was that he and his subordinates were exonerated. This bit of news greatly elated us, and in high spirits at the thought of freedom on the morrow I returned to my quarters, near the cow-gun, about 10 o'clock, where I was met by the officer in charge, who informed me that he had orders for me to move to the garrison prison there and then. After protesting against moving at such an unseemly hour, I had my bedding packed up and returned to the scene of our festival at the prison. I made a shakedown in Handcock's room, and turned in, fully expecting that this would be the last night of my imprisonment. The morning brought with it a rude awakening. At six o'clock Captain Brown, 2nd Wiltshire Regiment, came to the prison, and informed us that we were to entrain for Pretoria at 7 o'clock. We hastily got our kits together and had breakfast, when the Provost-Sergeant came to us carrying four pairs of handcuffs. After apologising for the unpleasant duty he was compelled to perform, he handcuffed us separately. When Morant held out his hands, he remarked, "This comes of empire building." His position then seemed to strike him very forcibly, for he broke down completely and wept.

We were then escorted under a guard with fixed bayonets to the station, and confined in two closed armoured trucks, Major Lenehan (who was not handcuffed), Lieutenant Morant and myself in one, and Lieutenants Handcock and Picton in the other. An officer and six men in each truck acted as guard. While waiting on the platform to

115

entrain, Major Bolton came up to us, as though to gloat over the successful consummation of his labours. Picton turned to him, and exposing the irons on his hands, called out, "I have to thank you for these, Major Bolton." Major Thomas had not been informed of our departure, and consequently did not travel with us. This was probably done to prevent any interference on his part; he followed on, however, shortly after.

Quite a crowd had gathered on the station, many laughing and joking as though it were a picnic excursion, others bewildered and wondering what was to be our fate. It appeared to me to be an insult to the British uniform we wore that we should undergo the indignity of being placed in irons before we were sentenced or deprived of our badge of rank. I could not think that our position called for such precautions, and held there must be some mistake, perhaps the result of officiousness on the part of the Provost-Marshal.

Leaving Pietersburg on the morning of 21st February, we arrived at Pretoria the following day, and were met by a strong escort of military police. Here we were placed in a van with armed men on either side of us, and with mounted police armed with revolvers and swords riding in the front and rear, and on both flanks. There were quite enough to form a bodyguard for the Commander-in-Chief himself.

With the exception of Major Lenehan, who was sent on to Capetown, we were driven to the old Pretoria Gaol. This was the first time I had ever been inside a civil prison. My first impressions were anything but encouraging; the warders appeared most uncivil. The first one we met told us in a domineering manner to "face the wall," then commenced to order us about. Morant resented this treatment; turning to him he said, "Look here, warder, recollect although I am a prisoner I am still a British officer, and will be treated as such."

On being taken to the reception room, we were stripped and our clothing carefully searched; we were then examined, and a complete description for identification purposes taken. Our own clothes were returned to us, and we were then taken to separate cells and locked up--in the quarters where Dr. Jameson and his followers had been confined after his disastrous and abortive raid on the Boer Republic a few years previous.

When the cell door closed behind me the thought came into my mind that for some underhand motive my position from the beginning had been falsely represented to me. I had treated it too lightly; gloomy forebodings as to the future then struck into my heart. Even then I could not believe that capital punishment would be meted out to any of us.

The following morning we were removed to another part of the prison, and occupied a row of cells on the west side of the yard, which I afterwards learned were known as the "condemned cells." During the day Captain Purland, Inspector of Prisons, visited us; he was an old acquaintance of Morant's, and at the request of this officer he relaxed much of the prison discipline. Instead of being kept locked in our cells all day, they were thrown open at 5.30 in the morning until 7 p.m. During the day we were allowed to associate with each other; tobacco, cigars, and cigarettes were sent to us, which we were permitted to smoke. We had been at Pretoria nearly a week before the findings of the court were made known.

We arrived there on Saturday, 21st February, and it was not until Thursday, 26th February, that we were called into the Governor's office and informed of our fate. We were walking about the yard as usual at 8 o'clock, Morant asking me the same question that he had asked me before, "What are they going to do with us? Do you think they will shoot us?" I scouted the idea of it, and tried to reassure him by saying that if they shot us they would require to go on shooting officers every day.

A warder then came to Morant and informed him that he was required at the Governor's office. He walked over, and in a few minutes returned. His face was deathly pale; he looked as though his heart had already ceased to beat. I exclaimed, "Good God, Morant, what is the matter?" "Shot to-morrow morning!" was the reply. Handcock was called next; when he returned he appeared quite unconcerned. "Well, what is it?" I asked. "Oh, same as Morant!" he wearily replied, as though he were tired of it all, and felt relieved that the end had came at last.

117

I was next called, and walked across the yard quite prepared for, and fully expecting, the same fate as the others. On being ushered into the Governor's office, I was taken before Captain Hutson, Provost-Marshal of Pretoria. Glancing at me he said, "George Ramsdale Witton, you have been found guilty of murder and sentenced to death." He paused for a time, as if to give me the full grasp of that sentence. He then continued, "Lord Kitchener has been pleased to commute your sentence to penal servitude for life." I was then marched out, feeling quite resentful because my sentence had been commuted, as I felt that death a thousand times would be preferable to the degradation of a felon's life; I had already suffered a dozen times over pangs worse than death.

Lieutenant Picton was the next called. He soon returned. "Well, what luck?" I asked. "Found guilty of manslaughter and cashiered!" was his reply. The appalling injustice of the sentences was a terrible blow to us.

Morant by this time had pulled himself together, and was his old self again. He requested to be provided with writing material, and immediately petitioned to Lord Kitchener for a reprieve. Handcock at the same time also wrote, asking neither mercy nor anything else for himself, but begged that the Australian Government would be asked to do something for his three children.

To Morant's petition there came a brief reply from Colonel Kelly, second in command at Pretoria, stating that Lord Kitchener was away on trek. He could hold out no hope of reprieve; the sentence was irrevocable, and he must prepare to bear it like a man. Handcock's letter was returned to him without an acknowledgment. At the same time I sent out two telegrams--one to Mr. Rail at Capetown, another to my brother in Australia. I was officially informed that they had been sent, via Durban, but I learned later that both had been suppressed.

During the day Major Thomas visited us; the terrible news had almost driven him crazy. He rushed away to find Lord Kitchener, but was also informed by Colonel Kelly that the Commander-in-Chief was away, and not expected to return for several days. He then begged Colonel Kelly to have the execution stayed for a few days until he could appeal to the King; the reply was that the sentences had already been referred to England, and approved by the authorities there. There was not the slightest hope. Morant and Handcock must die.

After sentence had been passed upon Morant, the Provost-Marshal asked him if he wished to see a clergyman. "No!" he replied, in his usual fierce and curt style; "I'm a Pagan!" Handcock, hearing of this, inquired, "What is a Pagan?" Upon being enlightened, he said, "I'm a Pagan, too!" Thus these two went out of this life believing there was no God. Little wonder either!

During the afternoon two warders were busily engaged in the workshop, not a chain away from our cells, making two rough coffins; we could hear them quite distinctly all the afternoon, and knew what they were doing. In the evening they could be seen in the prison yard, where they had been placed just outside the workshop door.

At four o'clock I was informed that I would leave for England at five the following morning. At six a hamper was sent in containing a nicely got-up dinner for four. We laid it out in my cell, but it was scarcely touched. After the awful events of the day we had no relish for a feast. It was the last meal that two of the company would partake of in this world. Morant remarked, "Not to be blasphemous, lads; but this is 'The Last Supper.'" At seven two warders came to lock up for the night. At the request of Morant, he and Handcock were allowed to pass their last night on earth together. At the last moment I bade Morant good-bye. He said, "It's hard lines and a sideways ending, thus being sacrificed as an atonement to pro-Boer sentiments. Good-bye, Witton; tell the 'Bulletin' people 'The Breaker' will write no more verse for them; I'm going into 'laager' in the morning."

Morant spent most of the night writing, and then wrote his last verse

In prison cell I sadly sit, A d--d crestfallen chappy, And own to you I feel a bit-- A little bit--unhappy.

It really ain't the place nor time To reel off rhyming diction; But yet we'll write a final rhyme While waiting crucifixion.

No matter what "end" they decide-- Quick-lime? or "b'iling
ile?" sir-- We'll do our best when crucified To finish off in style, sir?

But we bequeath a parting tip For sound advice of such men
Who come across in transport ship To polish off the Dutchmen.

If you encounter any Boers You really must not loot 'em, And,
if you wish to leave these shores, For pity's sake, don't shoot 'em.

And if you'd earn a D.S.O., Why every British sinner Should
know the proper way to go Is: Ask the Boer to dinner.

Let's toss a bumper down our throat Before we pass to heaven,
And toast: "The trim-set petticoat We leave behind in Devon."

At five the next morning, 27th February, I was roused by a
warder, who informed me that an escort was waiting for me as soon as
I was ready. I asked permission to say good-bye to Morant and Handcock. I was allowed to see them only through the small trap-door. I
clasped their hands through this for the last time, and could scarcely
stammer a good-bye. I was more unnerved at the thought of their hate-
ful death than they were themselves. They were calmly prepared to
meet their death, as they often had been before at times during the war.

I was then taken away to the Chief Warder's office, handcuffed, and handed over to an escort of Cameron Highlanders, who
took me to the railway station, thence to Capetown. At the prison gate
I passed a squad of Cameron Highlanders waiting to be admitted. It
was unnecessary to ask why or what they were there for. It was a
heart-breaking sight.

I was told that at six o'clock the warders threw open the door
of the doomed men's cell, and asked, "Are you ready?" "Yes!" replied
Morant, "where is your firing party ?" Hand in hand in the grey light
of the dawn they walked out to their death. To Lieutenant Edwards
Morant said, "Remember the Boers mutilated my friend Hunt. I shot
those who did it. We had our orders; I only obeyed them when Hunt
was murdered. I did it. Witton and Picton had nothing to do with it; I
told them so at the court-martial." They faced the firing party unflin-
chingly. While waiting at the Pretoria Railway Station I distinctly

heard in the clear morning air the report of the volley of the firing party, the death knell of my late comrades, and I knew they had gone to that bourne from whence no traveller returns. So went out two brave and fearless soldiers, men that the Empire could ill afford to lose.

It was Morant's last wish that he should be buried decently, and outside the precincts of the prison. Some comrades claimed the bodies, and interred them in the Pretoria cemetery; there Morant and Handcock went into their last long "laager." I shudder now as I write this and recall those awful days, so vividly impressed on my memory.

Those courts-martial were the greatest farces ever enacted outside of a theatre, and were held purely to conform to the rules of military law. The sentences were decided upon the evidence taken at the court of inquiry, at which no one was given an opportunity of making a defence, or even of denying the slanderous and lying statements made by prejudiced and unprincipled men. Morant and Handcock were sentenced to death long before the court sat to take evidence for the murder, or supposed complicity in the murder, of the said German missionary. It was not intended to seriously punish me, but a conviction in that case having been missed, it was necessary to include me to secure Handcock: For shooting Boers Captains Taylor and Robertson, Lieutenants Picton and myself, Sergeant-Major Hammett and the troopers were practically let off.

When Australians were waiting expectant and astounded for the truth concerning the terrible news that was coming through in dribbles--with its stories of outrage, robbery, and murders--this report was sent by Lord Kitchener to the Governor-General of Australia in reply to an urgent request for information, and was published in the Australian press on the 7th April, 1902, and throughout the civilised world:--

"In reply to your telegram, Morant, Handcock, and Witton were charged with twenty separate murders, including one of a German missionary, who had witnessed other murders. Twelve of these murders were proved. From the evidence it appears that Morant was the originator of the crimes, which Handcock carried out in cold-blooded manner. The murders were committed in the wildest part of the Transvaal, known as Spelonken, about eighty miles to the north of

Pretoria, on four separate dates, namely, 2nd July, 11th August, 23rd August, and 7th September. In one case, when eight Boer prisoners were murdered, it was alleged in defence to have been done in a spirit of revenge for the ill-treatment of one of their officers--Lieutenant Hunt--who was killed in action. No such ill-treatment was proved. The prisoners were convicted after most exhaustive trial, and were defended by counsel. There were, in my opinion, 'no extenuating circumstances.' Lieutenant Witton was also convicted, but I commuted the sentence to penal servitude for life, in consideration of his having been under the influence of Morant and Handcock. The proceedings have been sent home."

To show the effect of the above report, I extract a few comments from leading journals:--

"Argus," 29th March, 1902:--"The London reports do not mention the alleged provocation of the Capetown corps, whose officer was murdered and mutilated."

"Leader," 12th April, 1902:--"The War Office report, supported by the direct able message received by His Excellency the Governor from Lord Kitchener, Commander-in-Chief in South Africa, has removed any possibility of our laying this flattering unction to our souls. We are not even able to discover any plea of extenuation which would lessen the guilt of deliberate and despicable murder on the part of those who were principally concerned, and who have suffered the penalty of their crime. The explanation originally offered by those who professed to speak with some knowledge of the circumstances went to show that the shooting of the Boer prisoners was in the nature of retaliation for an outrage committed on a wounded British officer who was said to have been brutally done to death. This statement is still persisted in by Lieutenant Picton, one of the officers tried by court-martial, who, though found guilty of manslaughter, escaped with the minor punishment of being cashiered."

"Age," April, 1902:--"The suggestion that the Boers were killed in a spirit of revenge for the ill-treatment of Captain Hunt is also discounted by Lord Kitchener's statement that no such ill-treatment was proved, and that there were 'no extenuating circumstances.'"

"Adelaide Register," 13th June, 1904:--"The accused pleaded that the Boers in the district which they had to patrol were merely bands of marauders who had 'stripped and mutilated a brother officer, but Lord Kitchener reported that no such maltreatment could be proved."

"Leader," April, 1902:--"It is not conceivable that Lord Kitchener would have approved the sentence of death unless there was some reason shown for this unalterable punishment."

"Commercial Advertiser," New York, April, 1902:--"The impartial punishment of colonials by Lord Kitchener should check the torrent of abuse on the Continent against Great Britain."

The following is a true copy of the findings of the court, and furnishes a complete answer and direct contradiction to Lord Kitchener's statement that there were "no extenuating circumstances":--

CASE I.--VISSER CASE.

SENTENCE. The court sentence the prisoner Sentence.

Lieut. H. H. Morant, Bushveldt Carbineers, to suffer death by being shot. Death.

Signed at Pretoria this 29th of January, 1902. H. G. DENNY, Lieut.-Col., C. S. COPLAND, President. Judge Advocate.

RECOMMENDATION TO MERCY.

The court strongly recommend the prisoner to mercy on the following grounds:--

1. Extreme provocation by the mutilation of the body of Capt. Hunt, who was his intimate personal friend.

2. His good service during the war, including his capture of Field-Cornet T. Kelly in the Spelonken.

3. The difficult position in which he was suddenly placed, with no previous military experience and no one of experience to consult.

Signed at Pretoria the 29th day of January, 1902. Confirmed-- H. C. DENNY, Lt.-Col., KITCHENER, General. President. 25th February, 1902.

Promulgated at Pretoria, 26th of February, 1902, and extracts taken. Sentence carried out at Pretoria on the 27th February, 1902.

H. W. RUTSON, Asst. Prov. Marshal, Pretoria, 27th February, 1902. Pret. Dist.

EIGHT BOERS CASE.

SENTENCE. The court sentence the prisoners--Sentence. Lieut. H. H. Morant, Bushveldt Carbineers, to suffer death by being shot. Death.

Lieut. P. J. Handcock, Bushveldt Carbineers, to suffer death by being shot. Death.

Lieut. G. R. Witton, Bushveldt Carbineers, to suffer death by being shot. Death.

Signed at Pietersburg, this 4th of February, 1902.

H. C. DENNY, Lt.-Col., C. S. COPLAND, Major, President. Judge Advocate.

RECOMMENDATION TO MERCY.

The court recommend Lieut. H. H. Morant to mercy on the following grounds:--

Provocation received by the maltreatment of the body of his intimate friend, Capt. Hunt.

Want of previous military experience and complete ignorance of military law and military procedure.

His good service throughout the war.

The court recommend Lieut. P. J. Handcock and Lieut. G. R. Witton to mercy on the following grounds:--

1. The court consider both were influenced by Lieut. Morant's orders, and thought they were doing their duty in obeying them.

2. Their complete ignorance of military law and custom.

3. Their good services throughout the war.

Signed at Pietersburg this 4th day of February, 1902. H. C. DENNY, Lt.-Col., President.

I confirm the finding and sentence in the case of Lieuts. Morant and Handcock.

I confirm the finding in the case of Lieut. Witton, but commute the sentence to one of penal servitude for life.

25th February, 1902. KITCHENER, General.

Promulgated at Pretoria on the 5th February, 1902, and extracts taken. Sentence carried out at Pretoria on the 27th February, 1902.

H. W. HUTSON, Capt., Court Provost Marshal, Pretoria District. 27th February, 1902.

The 2nd July, the first date mentioned in Lord Kitchener's report, was the date on which six Boer prisoners were shot, when Captains Taylor and Robertson were in charge at Spelonken, and for the murder of whom Captain Taylor was tried and acquitted (details page 137).

125

The 2nd July Lieutenant Morant was not serving with the Spelonken detachment, and I had not then joined the Carbineers, but was at East London, in Cape Colony. There is one fact, however, and that is, no one has yet been punished for the shooting of the six Boers on the 2nd July.

The court-martial, after a most exhaustive trial, acquitted Morant and Handcock on the charge of shooting the German missionary (see Chapter XIX.).

CHAPTER XXI

"IMPRISONMENT FOR LIFE!"

The distinction between a trial by court-martial and a trial by civil court is illustrated by the trial of Barend Celliers, a Boer, for the murder of a British officer, which took place about twelve months after the trial of the Carbineers. I extract the following:--

"The trial of Barend Celliers, an Orange Free State field-cornet, for the murder of Lieutenant Boyle, a British officer, in 1901, was concluded at Bloemfontein. Celliers did not deny shooting Lieutenant Boyle, but pleaded not guilty on the ground that he had obeyed the orders of Commandant Philip Botha. General De Wet, who had previously held a court-martial on Celliers for shooting Lieutenant Boyle, and had acquitted him, gave evidence that Philip Botha, who had died some time ago, had expressed himself very strongly against Lieutenant Boyle, but he was not aware that Botha had ordered Boyle to be shot, though he might have done so without his knowledge. The jury acquitted Celliers."

Lieutenant Boyle was for a time the British officer in charge at Dewetsdorp, and for some reason or other became very obnoxious to the Boers of the town, the women especially hating him. Philip Botha, whose commando was in the neighbourhood, said to Celliers and others, "If ever we get Dewetsdorp again, I shall settle up with Lieutenant Boyle." When the town was recaptured Boyle was taken prisoner with other officers, but was kept separate from them. After he had been held a prisoner for about a week, Celliers went to his tent accompanied by another Boer, and ordered him out on the veldt. When some distance from the laager, Celliers (who said he had been ordered by Philip Botha to shoot him) informed Boyle that he had five minutes for prayer, and shot him in the back while he was still on his knees praying.

No court-martial or pretence of court-martial was ever held by the Boers upon Lieutenant Boyle, and no charge was ever made directly against him. When General De Wet inquired into the case he held Philip Botha responsible, and took no action because the latter was dead. The jury agreed with his decision.

These cases are sufficient to justify my belief that courts--martial and military tribunals should be speedily wiped out of existence. A trial by judge and jury, in an ordinary court, should never under any circumstances be departed from.

I left Pretoria on the morning of the 27th, and reached Nauuport about midnight. At 2 o'clock I was awakened by a crash and a sudden jolt, which almost threw me from the upper berth in which I was lying; the train then suddenly stopped. Upon inquiry from my guard I learned that our train had collided with another, stabled in the siding. Two carriages and the van were much splintered and derailed, and had to be switched off. This mishap delayed us about two hours.

We arrived at De Aar at midday on Saturday; here I tipped my guard to get me some lunch. Leaving De Aar we passed through the great Karoo desert, where for hundreds of miles, as far as the eye could reach, was the same monotonous view of bare kopje and barren veldt; the only vestige of herbage is the stunted karoo bush.

I passed through Matjesfontein, the model village of South Africa, the property of the Hon. J. D. Logan, who later figured prominently in the efforts that brought about my release. On reaching Capetown I was taken to the Castle Military Prison; there I met Major Lenehan, who was detained waiting embarkation for Australia. I informed him of the fate of his two officers, of which he was not aware. Lieutenant Picton was detained at the Castle, but not under the same restraint, he being permitted to go outside under escort. I sent for Mr.

Rail, the Government agent for Australian troops, and inquired if he had received my telegram from Pretoria; he said that he had not, nor had he received any news whatever regarding the affair. Upon acquainting him with the facts, he advised me to write out a statement of the case, which he would forward to the Victorian Government. He kept his promise; I know it was sent, and received by Sir Alexander Peacock, then Premier of Victoria.

The military authorities suppressed all knowledge of the findings of the court. While at Capetown I wrote several letters giving a brief account of the facts; I also sent another cable on the 8th March, which I paid for at ordinary rates, but all were suppressed. No knowledge of my fate reached my relatives, nor did any news regarding the affair reach Australia until Major Lenehan arrived in Melbourne on 25th March, a month after I had been sentenced. I was detained at the Castle some days, during which time I was kept under strict surveillance; on two occasions only was I allowed to be visited by friends from outside. Captain Baudinet, a brother officer, was refused permission to see me by the Provost Marshal and the headquarters authorities.

On the morning of 9th March I was taken on board the "Canada," lying at the South Arm Docks; two military police accompanied me, one of whom said to the regimental police sergeant, when handing me over, "Keep your eye on Witton; he'll try to escape if he gets a chance." I had not thought of doing any such thing; if I had wished to escape I could have done so long before. Morant was offered time and again at Pietersburg the opportunity of getting away; the best horses would be at his disposal outside the lines, and everything ready any time he wanted to go, but he would not take advantage of it. We all preferred to see it through.

I was placed in a small cabin in the guard-room, presumably for extra security; this proved to be a blessing in disguise. Before the boat sailed the guard-room was filled with drunken and rowdy troops. The first few days I fared rather badly, as I had to trust to the courtesy of the prisoners there to serve up my meals; I was more often forgotten than not. On the third day I asked to see the officer commanding the troops on board; he came to see me during the daily inspection. I told him how I was situated, and asked permission to have my meals sent from the saloon. This was granted, and I was allowed to make my own arrangements with the cook.

Lieutenant Picton, who was on board under no restraint, arranged everything satisfactorily. Afterwards, by making a chum of the police sergeant, I was provided with a servant for the rest of the voyage, and in the company of the sergeant I spent most of my time during the day on deck; I never then went short of anything that money could buy. I received the sympathy of all on board.

One day, while promenading on the deck, I was pointed out to a well-known British General, who was sitting on the bridge deck. "There's young Witton," a bystander remarked. "I know him, I know him; it's a d--shame; pity there isn't more like him in South Africa," burst out the General. There were over two thousand troops on board, and my situation was much discussed and commented upon. It was proposed to get up a petition there and then praying for a remission of my sentence, but I thought it quite unnecessary, as the Australian Government would be in receipt of all particulars of my case, and an investigation would probably be demanded before I reached England. I did not expect to be long a prisoner; in two months' time there would be the Coronation, and this I expected would bring liberty to all military prisoners.

My voyage to England, in spite of this, was not an enjoyable one. I was being taken away from my homeland into unmerited exile, a stranger in a strange land, branded as a criminal; these thoughts brought with them extreme mental pain and anxiety. After coaling at Las Palmas, during which time I was kept confined in my cabin, the "Canada" proceeded on her journey, and reached Queenstown on Easter Sunday. Here I got a glimpse of the Emerald Isle; being springtime, it did not belie its name. Queenstown has a magnificent harbour, far superior to anything I had then seen. The Irish troops who were on board, principally Cork militia, were disembarked. While in port I was handed an Irish newspaper, a pro-Boer journal, in which was published a long article headed "A Sad Tale from the Veldt." Its infamous statements were obviously the efforts of a malign imagination, as false as they were sensational, yet a recital of these was allowed to be published broadcast.

Lieutenant Picton, on his arrival in England, flatly contradicted these vile assertions, but it was an impossible task to suppress them when pitted against the ghoulish journalism of the world. South Africa was under martial law, and those who protested there became marked men, and ran a risk of being imprisoned on some trumped-up charge. Others, suspected of a desire to make disclosures, were silenced by a promise of an important post under the new administration. Such promises, although unofficial, had a good effect in the policy of suppression.

After leaving Queenstown the "Canada" headed for Southampton. I remained on deck until dark, hoping to see Morant's longwished-for beacon, "the Ushant light on the starboard bow," but the night was very foggy and the light was not in evidence. Passing up the Solent, past the Needles and close to the Isle of Wight, in Southampton Waters, we arrived at our destination about midday on 2nd April. Labels similar to those used by tradesmen when sending out goods were issued to us, inscribed with our number, name, and regiment, and we were instructed to attach them to our dress. It seemed a ridiculous farce for a man to have to label himself, but the motive in this case was, I was told, to assist the police in identifying and forwarding drunken Tommies to their destination. I still have my label in my possession.

During the afternoon, when the troops had all disembarked, an escort of marines came on board to take charge of the prisoners. I was again handcuffed, on this occasion with a young Imperial lieutenant, who emerged from among the Tommies in the guard-room.

We then entrained for Gosport. After leaving the train we travelled the last stage to the Gosport Military Prison in a waggonette. When the vehicle pulled up at the outer gate and set us down to await admission, I indulged in a few last whiffs of a cigarette. Whilst doing so I took a survey of the prison building, with its forbidding walls and long rows of small barred windows, and felt awed and chilled by the gloomy and silent air of the place--a foretaste of the life I was about to enter upon.

At last the wicket-gate was opened, and we filed through into a small courtyard; here the irons were removed from our aching wrists;

then, passing through more gates and stout doors, we entered the main hall, where strict silence had to be observed. We were here called up one by one before the Chief Warder.

While waiting I looked around me. There was a long corridor with three terraces of cells on either side, fronted with polished iron rails, a corkscrew staircase from the ground mounting to the heights above, and door after door passing into dim perspective.

When my turn came to go up, I was asked my rank, regiment, crime, and sentence, and was then told to hand over all personal property in my possession. Among the things I handed over were a dozen packets of cigarettes, which had been given to me by an officer on the "Canada." I was then taken to a bathroom, and after a good hot bath, a complete outfit of clothes of navy blue serge and other kit were given to me; I was then sent to cell No. 36 on the top landing. I walked into the cell, which appeared to be about 7 feet wide by about 13 feet long by 10 feet high, with a vaulted brick ceiling. In the cell was a small wooden table, a wooden stool, a bed board, three small mattresses of the biscuit pattern, a hard pillow, three army blankets, and a number of tin utensils.

I sat down on the stool and began taking a note of my surroundings. This, then, was to be my home for an indefinite period. I determined to try and make the best of everything, and settle down to the routine of prison life. My musings were suddenly disturbed by the gruff voice of a huge warder demanding why I did not close my door; I replied that I did not know it was my duty to close it, I had not been told to do so. After a long reprimand, I was given strict injunctions always to close my door when entering or leaving my cell.

Shortly after there was a rattle of tin cans outside, and a key in my door, which was thrown open. Supper was being served; I was handed a pint of oatmeal gruel and six ounces of dry white bread. This was my first meal in an English prison, and it was anything but gratifying.

When supper was finished the library warder came to me with a bundle of books, from which I chose Dickens' "Little Dorrit." Its tale of the old Marshalsea prison life interested me greatly. I read until locking-up time, which at Gosport was a quarter to eight. I was told that I must be in bed by eight o'clock, when the lights would be turned out. Though very tired, even in this abode of silence I could not sleep; I lay for hours thinking. They were the heaviest hours it was ever my lot to know; they were as weary as they were bitter. My hopes of a military career were irretrievably lost, my life blighted; I had been proclaimed to the world a felon, immured for a lifetime, and all brought about by the observance of the first duty of a soldier, "obedience to orders."

At midnight I became oblivious of everything, and was only awakened by the clang of the bell at half-past five. After washing, dressing, and arranging my bedding, my door was again flung open, and a warder and orderly came in with a bundle of short pieces of hard tarred rope. "I have brought you some work," said the warder. "Do you know how to pick oakum?" "I do not," I replied. "Very well, you will learn now." The orderly was then requested to instruct me in the art. Taking a strand of the rope, he rubbed it backwards and forwards on his knee, then taking it between his forefinger and thumb he frayed it into a woolly mass. He whispered to me, "These 'ere 'ard bits," showing a short length of hard dry rope, "yer want to 'ammer on the floor, but don't do it when there's anybody about, as 'e'll 'ear yer." I returned him my grateful thanks for his "tip," and promised to try it. I was then left with several pounds of rope, which was to be my task for the day.

Prior to my imprisonment my ideas of a convict's life centred round bread and water and picking oakum; they were almost realised. Sitting down, I commenced to unravel the awful stuff, but no matter how I tried I could not get it anything near as fine as the sample; to make matters worse, my fingers being tender, the tar commenced to burn them. For about an hour I worked steadily, until my shoulders ached and my fingers were almost raw.

Then came breakfast, my second prison meal, which consisted of the same amount of dry bread as for supper; three-quarters of a pint of cocoa was served in place of the gruel. By this time I felt hungry, and ate my loaf and drank my cocoa with eagerness. Then came again the banging and slamming of doors, the rattle of keys, and my own door was flung open. "Exercise. Close your door," shouted the warder. Leaving my cell, I hastened to the ground floor, where we fell-in in double file in the centre of the hall. When all were down we were called to "Attention," "Open order," "March." During this parade the Chief Warder made a daily inspection to see that every man had his uniform carefully brushed and his boots polished.

In single file we were marched out into the yard, and forming a circle walked round and round for an hour. Exercise over, I returned to my cell for a few minutes, then more unlocking and banging of doors, as the warder shouted "Prayers." I was then conducted to the chapel, where "divine service" was held--at least, that was what they called it. On week days it was usually conducted by a warder in a most perfunctory manner; the way the prayers were gabbled over, to my mind, bordered on profanity. While prayers were being said and the Litany intoned I have seen tobacco passed round from one to another, and one morning I heard the following conversation:--"Say, jock, how is it you are back so soon? What happened this time?" "I got drunk, and was run in, and broke out of barracks and punched the provost-sergeant," replied Jock.

Much the same methods prevailed in the other prisons where I was confined, excepting that the services were usually conducted by a chaplain. It is absolutely wrong to force prisoners to attend daily such a burlesque; that is, if these services are held with a view to softening the hearts of the wicked ones, and giving them an idea of living a better life. It affects them in two ways only--nine-tenths of them get hardened beyond any hope of redemption, the other tenth get softening of the brain or religious mania. Two good services held on Sunday in a reverent manner would be quite enough, and would have a good effect at least on the majority. It does not do any good to continually sing hymns like the following:--

"Have mercy, Lord, on me, As Thou wert ever kind, Let me, opprest with loads of guilt, Thy wonted mercy find.

"Wash off my foul offence, And cleanse me from my sin, For I confess my crime, and see How great my guilt has been."

The work of a prison chaplain is an extremely difficult one; besides being a thorough Christian, he requires to have a kind heart and some fellow feeling, also a large amount of tact and judgment, otherwise it would be better for all concerned if he never approached a prisoner. It is the duty of the chaplain of a convict prison to visit each prisoner separately in his cell at least twice a year.

The following incidents came under my notice while I was in prison:--The chaplain entered the cell of a young lad who had been in the navy, and was serving a sentence for attempting to strike an officer. The greeting the lad received from this man of God was, "Well, are you another of the rape cases?" The prisoner, who was standing with his cap on, indignantly replied that he was not, he was there for attempting to strike an officer in the navy. "Take your cap off when you speak to me," haughtily replied the chaplain. The prisoner removed his cap and threw it on the floor, and requested that he should be left alone; if he wished to see a chaplain he would make an application. "I can see you when I wish," said the chaplain, as he banged the door. This chaplain had more prisoners reported and punished than any prison officer.

Another chaplain at another prison, when going his round, entered a cell and found the prisoner with his head buried in his arms, sobbing; on returning from labour at dinner-time he had found a letter thrown on his bed containing the news of the death of his wife. "Well, my man, what's the matter with you?" asked the chaplain. When the prisoner had told him his bad news, he replied, "Ah, that is a common occurrence here." After delivering himself of that goodly measure of consolation he walked out. The same chaplain visited the hospital one morning, and came to a prisoner who had just been admitted after being examined by the medical officer. "What is the matter with you?" asked the chaplain. "I have neuralgia," answered the prisoner. "Very painful thing, very painful thing--that is, if you have got it," remarked the chaplain.

There are exceptions, of course, and it is possible sometimes to meet a sympathetic minister in the prisons, but if he followed after those I have mentioned above, his task of reform would be almost a hopeless one.

An avenue for the abuse of sacred rites is the administration of Holy Communion. I have seen some of the most depraved specimens of humanity, men without any sense of morality or probity, accept the

Sacrament, thinking by doing so to gain favour in the eyes of the prison authorities through the chaplain. Others will partake of it merely for the sup of wine. I know of one man who was advised to go to Communion; when he returned he said, "I have been to Communion; it was tip-top wine, too, but I couldn't get enough of it."

Prayers over, I went back to my cell and made a fresh start on the oakum. I had just settled down to this monotonous occupation when I heard another rattle of keys at my door, and the prison regimental sergeant-major came in. After a few cheery remarks, he asked me what work I had been put to. I told him. "I'll find you something more suitable than that," he said; "you can do some bookbinding, and write out a few lists for me; if there is anything you want, ask for it." "How often can I have a bath?" I asked. "You can have a hot one every morning; just ask your warder to send you down; if you don't get it, let me know," he replied. Without regarding the relative positions we occupied I thanked him for his kindness, and, as he was leaving, he told me the Governor wished to see me at dinner-time. That visit was like a ray of sunshine in my abode of gloom, and was productive of much that made the remainder of my stay at Gosport bearable.

Dinner was served at 12 o'clock. It consisted of a pint of soup, three-quarters of a pound of potatoes, and four ounces of bread. I had just finished my dinner when I heard someone shout out, "Send Witton down." My door was opened, and a warder told me I was wanted below. I went down, and was ushered into the Governor's office. The Governor appeared to be interested in my case, probably on account of what had been recently published; he asked me to tell him briefly how I came to be in my present position. I explained as briefly as I could how Captain Hunt met his death, and the unfortunate ending of Lieutenant Morant's command, and the part I had taken in it. "It was a case of retaliation, then," he observed.

After that interview I was treated with marked deference by the prison staff, and was allowed another hour's walking exercise during the afternoon. No restrictions regarding writing or receiving letters were enforced; my work now was merely an employment to kill time, and consisted of patching up old library books and writing out lists and forms. Sometimes, when my afternoon exercise was due, and it happened to be raining, I would be put on to cut up old rope into short

136

lengths; the hardest and dry pieces I would cut extra short, hoping that in doing so I would be serving some other unfortunate a good turn. I remained at Gosport Military Prison from the 2nd to the 26th April.

I was then transferred to Lewes, the Sussex County Civil Prison. On the morning of my departure from Gosport my khaki uinform was returned to me, and I was taken to Lewes in the same dress as that in which I arrived from South Africa.

CHAPTER XXII

GAOL DISCIPLINE AND PRISON BLUNDERS

The transfer from prison to prison is a most trying experience; manacled and chained, one is subject to the prying looks and embarrassing remarks of inquisitive spectators. My journey to Lewes was uneventful. I and a young private were escorted by a colour-sergeant and two men; they were jolly fellows, and had not been to South Africa. They could not understand how a man could be sentenced to life imprisonment for shooting Dutchmen. "Wasn't that what you went there for?" they asked; "it's terrible hard luck. Do you smoke, sir? These," handing me a packet of cigarettes, "are only common fags, but I'll get some better ones at the railway station." My sympathetic escort was true to his word, and when we entrained at Portsmouth Station he produced a packet of savoury "Egyptians."

We reached Brighton just as the London express arrived; its palatial cars and appearance of wealth and ease contrasted deeply with our war-worn uniforms and irons, and the gloomy destiny before us. We arrived at Lewes an hour earlier than we were expected, consequently, and luckily, there was no prison van to meet us. Hurrying off the platform, our escort requisitioned a "cabby," who drove us to the prison gate.

All main entrances are the same, and all prisoners are on an equality. First the massive outer gate is passed through into a gloomy, tunnel-like passage, with another and inner gate at the end, then across a portion of the prison yard to the reception cells. Here my committal warrant was carefully examined; the irons were then removed, and again a full description was taken, including my height and weight. I was then taken to the clothing department, and here I donned the degrading garb of the convict--a drab jacket and cap, and knee breeches, grey stockings, and leather shoes, freely stamped with the broad arrow. I was then taken to the main hall and placed in cell No. 35, which was similar to the one I had left at Gosport. I was here given a cloth badge, which buttoned on my left breast, and upon which was stamped A4/35, signifying the place and number of my location.

My dinner was then served, consisting of a small piece of boiled bacon and a quantity of haricot beans. In another small tin, which fitted into the one containing the beans and bacon, were a few black-looking potatoes, boiled in their jackets; on the top of these was a hard loaf of heavy brown bread. The only piece of cutlery was a wooden spoon. The meal did not present by any means a tempting appearance; the quantity was greater, but the quality was worse than the dietary at Gosport.

Dinner over, the schoolmaster' paid me a visit. After questioning me as to my religion, and tastes in regard to reading matter, he left me, and returned shortly after with a pile of books. Those I had asked for were not included, but he had brought a magazine, several educational works, and a slate. The titles and numbers of the books were entered on a library card which I kept in my cell.

Later on the chaplain came in; he was one of the exceptions in chaplains, and we had a long conversation. He expressed great astonishment at the severity of my sentence, and urged me not to worry too much about the future. He was my best friend during his short stay at Lewes; he visited me almost daily, and these visits were the only bright spots in that land of gloom and silence.

The outlook at Lewes was very far from cheering. I was put to picking oakum again, and was herded with the old offenders, or "old lags," as they are termed in the prisons. Being a first offender, I should have been placed in what is called the "star class," but I had first to furnish the Governor with the names of two persons who could vouch for my previous good character. As I knew no one in England sufficiently for the purpose, it was necessary to write to Australia, and three months elapsed before I was admitted to the "star class."

On the first morning after my arrival at Lewes, the crowning indignity of the prison service was enforced upon me. I had to submit to the operations of the barber. My hair was closely cropped all over with a pair of fine hair-clippers, and my face cleanly shaven; parting with my moustache seemed like parting with an old friend.

A copy of the rules and regulations of the prison service, to which a prisoner has to conform, is furnished to each, and is neatly printed on cardboard and kept in a small portfolio in the cell. These rules are so numerous and so lengthy that it is impossible to give them verbatim. The following is a short abstract:--

A prisoner shall at all times preserve unbroken silence.

He shall not communicate in any way with another prisoner except with the permission of one of the authorities.

He shall use no obscene language nor be guilty of any indecent act or gesture.

While in his cell or place of location he shall not make any unnecessary noise by singing, shouting, or whistling.

He shall not leave his cell or other place of location without permission.

He shall keep his cell and all prison property in his possession neat and clean.

He shall not have in his possession anything he ought not to have.

For mutiny or inciting to mutiny or personal violence on any officer or servant of the prison a prisoner will be liable to corporal punishment.

Should a prisoner have any complaint to make regarding his food, he must complain immediately it is issued to him. Repeated frivolous or unfounded complaints will be treated as breaches of prison discipline, and punished accordingly.

A prisoner must attend Divine service unless excused by the prison authorities.

No prisoner shall be compelled to worship in the form contrary to his religious convictions. In the case of Nonconformists a minister of the persuasion of the prisoner shall from time to time be permitted to visit him.

A prisoner should behave with reverence at Divine service.

He shall be employed on steady hard labour for a period of not less than ten hours per day, exclusive of the time allotted for meals.

A prisoner shall be permitted the use of a suitable library, educational and devotional books; if necessary, school instruction shall be administered.

He must conform to the rules of the prison regarding haircutting and bathing, as may be deemed expedient to health and cleanliness.

He may be allowed to interview the Governor to lodge complaints or make requests.

He may also be permitted to interview a director, inspector, or member of the board of visiting magistrates, or the board of magistrates, or any representative of the Home Office who may from time to time visit the prison. He may also be allowed to petition the Secretary of State.

Rules under the classification and remission system provide that:--

A prisoner's sentence shall be a question of marks, at the rate of six marks a day. He may, however, earn seven or eight marks a day, according to his industry and good conduct.

He shall be allotted marks according to the degrees of industry, seven marks for a fair, but moderate day's work, eight marks for a day's steady hard labour and the full performance of his allotted task.

A prisoner can thus by good conduct shorten his sentence by one-fourth.

A prisoner under sentence for penal servitude for life must not expect his release until he has completed twenty years' imprisonment, nor will any number of marks be taken to represent his sentence. However, his marks earned will be recorded, and in due time considered by the Secretary of State.

A prisoner for ill-conduct or any breach of prison regulations may forfeit any number of marks or the whole of his remission.

A prisoner having earned the number of marks representing his sentence will be released on license for the remainder.

His period of incarceration will be divided into stages (or classes). In the first, or probationary, stage, he must pass one year or until he has earned 2920 marks. During the first six monhts of his sentence, or until he has earned 1460 marks, he will be kept in separate confinement and be employed not less than ten hours per day, exclusive of time allotted for meals. He may be permitted to write or receive a letter during the first week of his sentence, and for every 960 marks earned in this stage he will be accorded the privilege to write and receive one letter and receive a visit of twenty minutes duration, or write and receive a letter in lieu of a visit by not more than three friends or relatives. When he has earned 1460 marks in this stage he will be eligible to be transferred to a public works or convict prison.

During the second stage he will be allowed the same privilege regarding writing and receiving letters and visits. He is to receive a gratuity of one shilling for every 240 marks earned in this stage, and will be distinguished by a narrow black cloth band on his sleeve, at the wrist and on the collar.

In the third stage he is permitted to write and receive a letter and receive a visit for every 720 marks earned, with the option of 2 oz. additional bread, 1/2oz. margarine in place of porridge, and a half-hour additional exercise on Sundays. He is distinguished in this stage by yellow facings, and he may earn a gratuity of one shilling and sixpence for every 240 marks, but not more than eighteen shillings while in this stage.

In the fourth stage he is permitted to write and receive a letter and a visit of thirty minutes' duration for every 480 marks earned, and to receive a gratuity of 2s. 6d. for every 240 marks, but not to exceed thirty shillings. He is distinguished by blue facings, and may be permitted to converse with a companion, selected by the Governor, during exercise on Sunday afternoon. In this stage a prisoner remains until the last year of his sentence. By continuous good conduct he is then eligible for the special class, the highest class of prisoners; its privileges are a blue uniform, a letter and visit every month, and the preference of any so-called privileged posts, such as infirmary or schoolmaster's orderly, also an extra gratuity of #3 should he join a prison aid society. He may be recommended for an extra remission not exceeding one week.

A prisoner serving a sentence of seven years or over can earn #6; he can earn no more if he undergoes a life sentence. This money is paid to him by the police under whose surveillance he is while on license or ticket-of-leave.

The greatest of all privileges is the red collar, usually given to a special class prisoner (very rarely to one in any other stage) when employed on any special work, such as painting or charging the furnace at the foundry. Then he is allowed to go about the prison unaccompanied by a warder. Greater trust is placed in these men, as they have so much to lose, and a breach of confidence is not so likely to occur.

I had now commenced on the probationary stages of my sentence and for three long, heart-breaking, soul-killing days I picked oakum. The master-tailor then came to my cell, and I asked for other work. "I do not care how laborious it might be," I told him, "I will do anything but pick oakum." "Can you sew?" he inquired. "Yes!" I eagerly replied, though the art of needlework as far as I knew it was sewing on a button.

I was brought a pair of scissors, two needles, a thimble, and the pieces of a prison jacket; after being shown how to place them together, I commenced work. I put the thimble on the wrong finger, but notwithstanding this, and the drawback of continually stitching my finger to the material, I made very good progress, and was kept at this work during my sojourn at Lewes.

The routine became more and more monotonous as time dragged slowly on. My constitution was practically run down with the two years on active service; then came the close confinement, the foul and fetid atmosphere, and the disgusting sanitary arrangements. It is little wonder that I left Lewes in broken health.

About a month after my arrival at Lewes I petitioned through the Secretary of State to Lord Roberts, the Commander-in-Chief, stating my case, and asking for a remission of the sentence. In course of time a reply came, which was brought to me by the Governor. It was to the effect that the Commander-in-Chief declined to make any remission of my sentence. This was a great blow to me, and seemed almost brutal in its significance. However, I hoped that the approaching Coronation would bring relief.

Coronation day came at last, and instead of the long-looked-for freedom, every prisoner was given a special treat, and made the recipient of the King's bounty in the shape of a slice of plum pudding. I was then told by a warder that the Coronation had been suddenly postponed owing to the serious illness of His Majesty. I was also told that the war had terminated, and peace had been declared, and that the Boer Generals were visiting England as guests of the nation; also of the doings of the Australian cricketers.

These items of news came like a ray of sunshine into my gloomy cell, raised my spirits, and tended to make life bearable, though it was very far from being worth living. Towards the end of June the necessary references as to character were forthcoming, and I was now transferred to the "star class," the division in which first offenders are kept apart from ordinary prisoners, and distinguished by a red star on each arm between the elbow and shoulder, and another on the front of the cap.

The "star" receives no privilege other than those granted to the old offenders, and is subject to a more rigid discipline. This step brought with it no change of work; I was still kept at the same sedentary labour in my cell. I had expected much as the result of the change--a relaxation of discipline, more humane treatment, better food, outdoor labour, and other advantages; but I hoped in vain.

I found great pleasure in reading, and I read as I worked anything and everything that was brought to me. At other times I would have put a lot of it aside as "dry," which I now simply devoured. Carlyle's works and essays fascinated me, causing me to forget my anxiety and troubles for the time being. Towards the end of my "separate," as this part of a prisoner's sentence is termed, I became morose and low-spirited. Nearly six months had passed, and my release seemed as far off as ever. Changes had taken place in the prison; a new Governor and chief warder had superseded the old ones, so I interviewed the new Governor for permission to petition again. My request was refused, and I was informed that, as I was a court-martial prisoner, I could only petition at intervals of not less than three months. This I considered hard and unfair, as it actually meant that I was not entitled to the same privileges as ordinary offenders.

I was determined not to let the matter rest. I interviewed every Home Office official that visited the prison--prison inspectors, directors, and boards of visiting magistrates. To all I pleaded to be allowed to petition direct to His Majesty the King, but I was informed that such a procedure was impossible, that the Home Secretary was the highest power on earth a prisoner could appeal to. I must wait a little longer, and petition again.

One day, about the end of July, just at the time when I was hopefully expecting to hear something regarding my release, two warders came to my cell, and threw open my door. One of them requested me in a cheery kind of way to bring out my clothes and bedding. What could it mean? Had my release come at last? Gathering up the things, I carried them out on to the landing, where they were carefully examined. I then had to gather them up and take them back to the cell again; here everything had been overhauled and thrown about. I was next requested to take off what I was wearing; these things also were carefully examined, and handed back to me. "That will do, get into them again," said the warder, as he walked out and closed the door. To my dismay, I found this was my first experience of the system of searching, or "having the bailiffs in," as it was called in the prison.

About the middle of August my hopes were again raised, and as suddenly shattered. On this occasion the Governor sent for me; I was required at his office. On entering, I noticed two footmarks painted on the floor in front of his desk, and pointing in the prescribed military angle of 45 degrees. These I was requested to stand upon, and was then asked by the Governor to give my register number and name. "Your six months' separate confinement is completed on Monday next," he said, "and you will be transferred to Portland Convict Prison." Then he added: "There are a number of letters for you accumulated here, which you are not entitled by prison regulations to receive. What am I to do with them?" No mention of freedom, and, what I prized next, my letters were denied me. "Do with them?" I said. "Considering they are letters from Australia, most of them written before I was convicted, and forwarded from South Africa, can you not do the same as your predecessor? Let me read them and return them to you to be destroyed." I urged and entreated to be allowed to receive them; I had had no news from the homeland for over two months; but no, the new Governor was inexorable; I must abide by the rules of the prison. So, after requesting that the letters be sent with my clothes to my friends, I went back to my cell more depressed than ever. The following day I was photographed for future identification, front and profile being taken. On Monday morning I and three other prisoners were manacled and chained together; two warders took charge of us, and in the prison brake we were taken to the station and entrained for Portland. I had heard glowing accounts of the prison there; it was the next best place to Parkhurst, the convalescent station in the Isle of Wight. The discipline was less stringent, there was better food and more of it, and mostly outdoor labour. Our escort officers were fairly lenient and good fellows. Portland was reached about six o'clock in the evening.

Arriving at the prison we were admitted and the irons removed. We were taken to the reception cells, where we changed our clothes. Supper was then served, a pint of fatty cocoa and a 12-Oz. loaf of coarse brown bread; then to bed. I slept very little during the night, and was awake when the bell rang out at 5.30 in the morning. For breakfast the liquid refreshment was alleged tea, a black, vile-looking concoction, sweetened with molasses, which robbed it of any flavour it may have possessed, and a 10-oz. loaf.

A warder then came and conducted me to the bathroom, afterwards to the tailor's shop, where I was fitted with new clothes. The shoemaker was then visited, and I was provided with a pair of heavy iron-shod boots for outdoor wear, and a pair of light shoes for Sunday. Afterwards came the visit to the medical officer at the infirmary, where I was examined, sounded, and weighed. It was now almost dinner time, the bell had rung, and parties of prisoners were being marched on to the parade ground from all directions. I was hurried back to the reception cells and taken before the Governor, Major Briscoe, who spoke kindly to me, and gave me a few words of very sound advice.

Returning to my cell, I found my dinner waiting for me--a lump of fat, tough "Dorset tup" mutton, with half a pint of the liquor it had been boiled in, a few potatoes, and an 8-oz. loaf of bread. I had my dinner, and waited, wondering what would be the next item on the programme. After a little time I was again conducted below and stripped. A most minute description was then made for future identification; every small scar and mark was recorded. Having now got through all the preliminaries, I was ready to be "located." During the evening I was taken to the "star" ward, F North Hall. Here I was placed in a cell which would not make a decent dog kennel; its dimensions were 3 ft. wide, 7 ft. long, 7 ft. high. A small window of opaque glass beside the door admitted light from a gas jet outside. A canvas hammock slung from end to end of the cell monopolised more than half its space; a small drop table, 12 X 15 in., which hung from the wall, and a wooden stool, with the usual cell utensils, completed the furniture. This, then, I mused, was my new home, in which I was practically to pass my lifetime; the outlook was anything but cheering. The chaplain came to see me, took down a few notes regarding my case, and prevailed upon me to join the choir.

I slept badly that night, and in the morning my head ached; I had no appetite; I just ate a little of the crust of my loaf. At seven o'clock my door was thrown open; standing in the doorway and glancing along the hail, I recognised many faces I had seen at Lewes, also my three companions of the trip down. We then fell in, in double file, and marched to chapel for morning prayers, for which about fifteen minutes was allowed. The General Confession or the Litany was intoned on these occasions. After chapel we were marched back to the parade ground, and as I had not yet been posted to any party, I was called out by the principal warder and afterwards conducted to No. 3 party, where I was engaged in tinsmithing and foundry work.

The pronounced opinion of the general public is, I believe, in favour of reforming the present English prison system. Thinkers who do not especially class themselves as philanthropists affirm the necessity of classifying prisoners so as to conserve any good that remains part of a man's character at the time of his committal to prison.

The object of imprisonment is so to punish a criminal that the punishment will act as a deterrent on him in the future, and check others who might be disposed to menace society.

From observations made while in prison I am of the opinion that many of the present methods of dealing with prisoners are calculated to increase crime, rather than to repress it.

Criminals should be divided into three classes--Habitual, Ordinary, and First Offenders. Each class should be kept apart, but this cannot be accomplished by confinement in one common prison. In England those belonging to the first offenders, or "star class," are placed in the same prison as the old offenders, but are not supposed to come in contact with them. Yet they work together in the same yard, though in different parties, and at times prisoners move about indiscriminately, and talk to each other. Warders differ much in disposition, and some, less strict than others, allow the contact that the arrangements are designed to prevent.

Less supervision would be needed if prisoners were graded and confined in separate prisons.

On one occasion, with a party of the "star class," I was returning from labour. Turning a corner, we came suddenly upon a party of "old lags" working on a tram line. Our warder peremptorily ordered us to turn "right about," in which position we still faced the remnant of another party of a similar class. The warder, taking in the serious nature of the situation, facetiously gave us the order, "Shut your eyes!" The undesirables were then quickly mustered and hustled out of our way.

The treatment of first offenders is of the utmost importance. Great discrimination should be used in dealing with men convicted for a first offence; these should be systematically sorted and graded, and kept at work in separate parties.

Among the first offenders, with whom I had the most experience, I was brought in contact with some of the most depraved specimens of humanity that could be found inside or outside of any prison. I also met men with refined feelings and instincts, to whom a sentence of a few months would be a more severe expiation than a long term to those before-mentioned.

If a man of previous good character be awarded a long term of imprisonment, he should be allowed to serve the greater part of it on license, under police surveillance, on recognisances of such a nature as would act as a check on his predatory instincts, at the same time giving him the opportunity of regaining his position as a useful and respectable citizen.

Ordinary prisoners, or those serving a second or third sentence, while kept in confinement should be allowed to earn a remission of a part of their sentence by industry and good conduct; this would also be an inducement for a rebellious prisoner to conform to prison discipline.

Habitual offenders, or those who make crime an occupation when at liberty, should be kept confined on an indeterminate sentence in an institution specially provided for them. The discipline should not be too rigid; they should be kept at some kind of reproductive work, and in return receive a small gratuity per month, which they might be allowed to spend on any extras in food or whatever they wished for themselves. These men should only be allowed at large when a tribunal that has based its opinions on scientific principles is satisfied that the prisoner's reformation is accomplished.

There are many classes of work on which prisoners could be employed, such as making bricks and other building material, also smelting and moulding iron, thus providing, the first essentials for an extension of a railway system.

The labour of prisoners made use of in such reproductive work should be supervised by artisan warders.

The "silent system," or the suppression of speech, is undoubtedly as a punishment an unqualified success. Suppression of speech, together with the gloomy surroundings, the petty and trivial annoyances to which prisoners are subjected from officious warders, and the enforced daily attendance at religious instruction, which usually terminates with a dirge-like hymn, is the cause of many prisoners developing symptoms of mental weakness.

A long sentence under the silent system is more inhuman than the brutal treatment awarded to prisoners in early Australian convict days. Some natures it will brutalise and train in crime; others it will wreck physically and mentally. The result in the former case means a return to crime and prison; in the latter a committal to an asylum or workhouse. In either case the victims become a burden on their country for the remainder of their days.

The "silent system" should be reserved and applied only as a punishment to refractory prisoners.

CHAPTER XXIII

THE PETITION FOR RELEASE

When on parade, the men in a party were always placed according to their height. I thus became a leading file, as I was the tallest man in the prison, standing a trifle over 6 ft. 2 in. in my prison boots. After taking my allotted place in the party, the process of searching was gone through. I was ordered to unbutton my coat, vest, and breeches at the knee, take my cap in my right hand, and my handkerchief in the left, and hold them out at arms' length while an officer passed his hands over my body. This search is carried out four times a day, on going out and returning from labour. When the search is over, and the coast clear--that is, when the old offenders are out of the way-- the "stars" march out past the saluting base, where stand the Governor and chief warder, whose duty it is to take down the number of men in each party. The number returning from labour must correspond with the number passed out to labour. The cell is also searched every night before locking up.

Once a month a prisoner is subjected to what is known as a "dry bath." The whole party is marched from the works to the bathroom, and one by one put into an empty bath and subjected to a private bodily search. The Portland workshops are situated about a quarter of a mile away from the prison, and are fairly extensive, nearly one hundred men being employed at tinsmithing and foundry work alone. I was now put on to learn soldering tinware. I soon mastered this art sufficiently to do practical work, and was engaged in making all the kinds of tinware used in the prison service, and biscuit tins and oil bottles for the navy.

For two days I kept at this work among the acid fumes. My appetite had now almost vanished; I hardly slept at all, and one of my boots had crippled me; I kept up, however, thinking that my indisposition was the result of the change of surroundings. On the third morning I felt very ill and quite unfit for work; I then made an application to see the doctor in the usual way, which necessitated waiting until the dinner hour and parading with the "reporting sick." I went out to work, but as soon as I started I felt dizzy and faint; I went to the warder in charge, and asked to be allowed to rest a little. He, seeing that I was ill, ordered me to be taken to the infirmary at once. I was escorted there by an assistant-warder, and admitted.

I was greatly struck by the beautiful cleanliness of the hospital; as I toiled up to the "star" ward, I noticed that the railings were polished like burnished steel, the cells were roomy and scrupulously clean, and in each were an iron bedstead, a table, and chair. The walls were painted a pale green on white, the floors were carpeted with coir matting, the passages with stout canvas, the whole building seemed as silent as the grave. I had not long to wait before the medical officer came in. I described my symptoms, and drew his attention to my foot. After examining me, he remarked, "A touch of influenza." Turning to the warder-nurse, he ordered me a dose of ether and ammonia, and a lead lotion dressing for my foot. I was then ordered to bed, where I remained for eight days; by that time my health appeared to have improved, and my foot was well again.

I was discharged from the hospital with a highly-prized concession--boots to measure, without nails. I felt very weak when leaving, and could scarcely walk; I was quite knocked up on reaching the hall, about 200 yards distant. I was again pigeon-holed in my 3 x 7 cell on the basement. The following day being Sunday, I had another rest, with one hour's exercise. The following week dragged on; I could neither eat nor sleep, and my head ached as though it would split. Cramped up in my narrow cell, in a hall in which were nearly 200 prisoners, with an atmosphere which words fail to describe, I rapidly became seriously ill. I kept on with my work until Friday, when I again applied to see the doctor. I went out as usual with my party, and was working on zinc, using "live acid." The fumes almost suffocated me; my head reeled, and for a time I became oblivious of everything. On coming round, I shivered as though suffering from ague; I was again hurried away to the hospital.

I thought I was suffering from malarial fever, and told the doctor so. I believe I was treated for that complaint for nearly a week, but I gradually became worse. My case puzzled both the hospital doctors; so one day samples of my blood were taken and forwarded to the Institute of Pathological Research for examination. A reply at once came back that the case was typhoid fever.

I was then removed to the end of the ward, isolated and quarantined, and screened off by two sets of carbolised sheets. My condition was considered to be very critical; I was dieted on peptonised milk, Valentine's meat juice, and a little brandy.

For nine long weeks I lay hovering over the fine line between life and death; I was so weak I could not raise my hand. Just as the last feeble spark of life seemed about to flicker out I rallied slightly, but did not make any progress. I could not sleep, and opiates had no effect upon me. The day warder-nurse who attended me told me afterwards that often, when he went off duty at night, he never expected to see me alive in the morning.

About 7 o'clock one morning I had my breakfast of milk, and do not remember anything more; I must have dropped into sound sleep. When I awoke the nurse was standing near. He said, "Oh! you are awake at last; what time do you think it is ?" "About nine o'clock!" I replied. "Well, it is five o'clock in the evening, and I have two pints of milk, a pint of beef tea, and two lots of brandy waiting for you; which will you have first ?"

From then I slowly improved. Though so close to death, it rarely, if ever, troubled my head; thoughts of my freedom and return to Australia, my native land, were always paramount.

One day, just after I had turned the corner, and was on the road towards recovery, I received from my brother in Australia a copy of the opinion of the Hon. Isaac Isaacs, K.C., and also a copy of the

Australian petition to His Majesty the King, which had been based on the opinion, and which I was informed was being supported by tens of thousands of His Majesty's subjects. It was a clear and truthful summary of my case. I read and re-read it, and felt that my release was assured; such a petition could not be long refused. The following is a copy:--

AUSTRALIA. The humble petition of the undersigned, your Majesty's most loyal subjects, Sheweth:--

1. Prior to May, 1900, George Ramsdale Witton was a gunner of the Royal Australian Artillery, in the service of the Crown in the Defence Forces of the colony of Victoria, Australia. He was born on the 28th day of June, 1874, and is now twenty-eight years of age.

2. On or about 1st May, 1900, the said Witton left Australia for South Africa with the Imperial Australian Regiment, under Lieutenant-Colonel Kelly, with the intention and purpose of serving in the military forces of the Crown against the Boers.

3. After being some time in South Africa he offered his services as a member of the Irregular Corps of the Bushveldt Carbineers, and was accepted, receiving, in consequence of his previous knowledge and practice of artillery, and notwithstanding his inexperience as an officer up to that time, a commission as lieutenant in that corps. He joined the corps on 13th July, 1901.

4. On 5th August, 1901, he joined the Spelonken detachment of the corps, then under the command of Captain Hunt. Captain Hunt, however, with the main body of the Spelonken detachment, when Lieutenant Witton arrived, was some miles away engaging the enemy, and was killed on 7th August. Lieutenant Witton never saw or had communication with Captain Hunt, but was always under the immediate command of Lieutenant Morant, as superior officer, and Lieutenants Handcock and Picton, all of whom were senior to Lieutenant Witton.

5. Lieutenant Witton is at present a prisoner of the Crown at Lewes, England, under sentence of penal servitude for life, by way of commutation by the General Commanding Officer, Lord Kitchener, of

a sentence of death by court-martial, upon the trial of Lieutenant Witton on two charges of murder of Boers.

6. No official copy of the proceedings is at present obtainable in Australia, but reliable information has been collected from reports in public newspapers, notably in the weekly edition of the "Times" for 18th April, 1902, and from persons having actual knowledge of the events, and from communications from Lieutenant Witton. From these sources the following circumstances appear to be those connected with the two cases in question.

7. The first charge was that of murdering a Boer named Visser. Visser was captured wounded shortly after Captain Hunt's death. Lieutenants Morant, Handcock, Picton, and Witton had a consultation with reference to Visser, and after that Visser was summarily shot, without trial and without charge. When captured he wore a soldier's khaki jacket or shirt, and was in possession of a pair of Captain Hunt's trousers. Although found guilty of the charge by the court-martial, your Majesty's petitioners humbly urge that for the reasons following no guilt in respect thereof is properly imputable to Lieutenant Witton.

8. He was the junior subaltern. He had so recently joined the corps and the detachment that he could not have personal knowledge of the material facts hereinafter mentioned. It was within a week of his joining the detachment that Visser's case occurred. Lieutenants Morant and Handcock had been for some time (over a month) under the direct control of Captain Hunt, and, therefore, in a position to know exactly what orders he had given and transmitted. The first witness for the prosecution--Sergeant S. Robertson--admitted in cross-examination that Captain Hunt had given direct orders that no prisoners were to be taken, and had also on one occasion abused the witness for bringing in three prisoners without orders. Lieutenant Morant deposed that not only had Captain Hunt given these orders, but also that he had named his authority, Colonel Hamilton. It is true that at the court-martial Colonel Hamilton proved that no such orders had been issued, but that, as your Majesty's petitioners humbly urge, could not be known to Lieutenant Witton at the time Visser was shot. If Captain Hunt informed his subordinates that Colonel Hamilton had given such orders, and Captain Hunt directly required obedience to them, it is humbly submitted that Lieutenant Witton had no course open to him as a soldier but to

obey. The order and the interpretation of that order were not left in any doubt according to the statements of his superiors. It is humbly further submitted that Lieutenant Witton would have much exceeded his right, would have been insubordinate, and as an officer been guilty of a serious dereliction of duty if he had ventured to demand from his superior officer proof of the truth of his statement as to the issue and meaning of the orders in question before yielding obedience, because if justified in demanding such proof from Lieutenant Morant, such demand might, as it seems to your Majesty's petitioners, be equally demanded from every officer short of the General commanding.

Your Majesty's petitioners humbly submit there was no criminality in a young and comparatively inexperienced lieutenant, with no previous experience in the field, less than a month with his corps, less than a week with his detachment, placing faith in and yielding obedience to the distinct assurances and positive commands of two superior officers, having vastly better means of knowledge, and with all the advantage and power of rank and authority.

We also rest reliance on the circumstances of time and place, which seem to be of the highest importance. At a great distance from still higher authority, even had he been disposed to question the authenticity and construction of his orders, immersed in services of continuous activity and serious pressure, engaged with an enemy whose methods, in some instances at least, as is well known, lent some colour to the likelihood of such orders, and having no reason for disbelieving what he was told, and led by a masterful mind and strong personal force, your Majesty's petitioners beg your Majesty's most gracious consideration to the difficult position of this young and inexperienced officer. Lieut. Colonel Pratt, in his "Handbook on Military Law," at page 113, says:--"A soldier, again, is bound to obey the lawful command of his superior officer, and before a court-martial it would be held that a soldier was bound to obey the command of his superior officer, if the illegality of it was not on the face of it apparent." Clode's "Military and Martial Law," at page 56, states that "The power and responsibility of the superior officer, i.e., the senior officer of the highest rank present, is always supreme."

No doubt can ever have existed, as your Majesty's petitioners believe, that Captain Hunt had given the orders referred to. Civil-

Surgeon Johnson testified that he had heard Captain Hunt reprimand Lieutenant Morant for bringing in prisoners; so did Captain Taylor. Collateral corroboration that Captain Hunt believed that such orders were justified appears also from the evidence in other cases as to the practice in other corps.

9. The second charge of which Lieutenant Witton was found guilty was called the eight Boers case. He was indicted, along with Lieutenants Morant and Handcock, with having murdered or instigated the murder of eight prisoners. The facts were that about 20th August, 1901, an intelligence officer named Ledeboer, in charge of a party, captured the Boers and handed them over to a patrol. On 23rd August they were shot. So far as Lieutenant Witton is concerned, he was present with others, but did not take part in any decision regarding the fate of the men. One of them rushed at him and seized hold of him, and then Lieutenant Witton shot him, apparently to protect himself. He neither ordered nor participated in the shooting of the other seven.

The prosecution proved that Lieutenant Morant again asserted his orders as his justification, and also stated he had been congratulated by headquarters over the last affair, and meant to go through with it. Clearly, as your Majesty's petitioners submit, Lieutenant Morant took command of the situation and exerted his authority.

The defence of obedience to orders, and the view that Lieutenant Witton honestly and reasonably believed in the existence of lawful orders, were, as your Majesty's petitioners believe, materially corroborated and supported by evidence in other cases before the same court-martial, that other corps believed the same thing and acted accordingly. Lieutenant Hannam stated that when he was a trooper in the Queensland Mounted Infantry, on one occasion at Bronkhurst Spruit, in 1900, his squadron took some prisoners and was reprimanded by Colonel Cradock for taking them. Sergeant Walter Ashton deposed to Brabant's Horse receiving orders to take no prisoners, in consequence of specific acts of treachery on the part of the Boers. Your Majesty's petitioners humbly submit that such reprimand and orders could have but one meaning, and that they afford strong reason for not imputing criminal conduct to Lieutenant Witton.

10. Lieutenant Witton states, in a letter of 8th March, 1902, that Sergeant-Major Clarke asked him to intercede with Lieutenant Morant on behalf of the men (British) in favour of Visser, that he agreed with the men that Visser should not be shot, and mentioned it to Lieutenant Morant. Lieutenant Morant, he says, refused to grant his intercession, telling Lieutenant Witton he was justified in what he was doing, and saying that if the men made any fuss he would shoot the prisoner himself.

11. Your Majesty's petitioners, while believing that, under the circumstances hereinbefore appearing, Lieutenant Witton ought not to have been punished as a criminal, desire to place before your Majesty further considerations which they humbly submit should move your Majesty's clemency towards Lieutenant Witton.

12. These circumstances are as follows:--Early on the morning of 23rd January, 1902, and while the court-martial was still in course of trying the prisoners at Pietersburg, an attack on the town by Commandant Beyers took place. So far as your Majesty's petitioners can learn, Lieutenant Witton, then under arrest, but under no personal danger from the Boers, was ordered and permitted to, and did, resume his arms, and until the attack was happily repulsed stand ready if needed to do honourable and perilous service in his country's and your Majesty's cause. Your Majesty's petitioners, while acknowledging that by your Majesty's regulations, such circumstances were not technically or necessarily an answer to the charge, if the same were otherwise established, do nevertheless most earnestly beg your Majesty to graciously regard them as of sufficient weight to induce your Majesty to pardon Lieutenant Witton.

At one period of the history of the British Army such circumstances would have been considered as almost equivalent to condonation. Clode, at page 103, states the general principle thus:-- The discharge of duty involves condonation, and quotes the Duke of Wellington as writing:--"The performance of a duty of honour and trust after the knowledge of a military offence committed ought to convey a pardon," and the author adds that, according to the practice of the Duke of Wellington in the Peninsula, it did so. That such was the practice of so distinguished a commander at a period of our history noted for the rigour of military discipline appears, we think, from a perusal among other sources of the despatch of the Duke of Wellington of 11th April, 1813, and the general order of His Grace dated 11th February, 1811.

13. Your Majesty's petitioners, without desiring to rest their prayer upon any technical grounds, would humbly beseech your Majesty to consider whether Lieutenant Witton has not suffered some disadvantage in not having as one member at least of the court-martial an officer of an irregular corps in accordance with the Rules of Procedure.

Reviewing the whole of Lieutenant Witton's unfortunate case, your Majesty's petitioners venture humbly to express to your Majesty the confident hope that your Majesty may perceive room and occasion for royal clemency.

Now that peace has been happily re-established, now that our late foes have been enrolled as our fellow-subjects, when even rebels have sought leniency, and not in vain, we approach the Throne asking that your Majesty may be graciously pleased to direct the liberation of the young and inexperienced soldier who, at an anxious moment of our history, ardently offered to his country the last gift of a brave and loyal citizen, and who, if, contrary to the views of your Majesty's petitioners, he erred at all, he erred, we venture most humbly and earnestly to submit, not from wilfulness or design, but, according to the great weight of testimony and probability, from a mistaken sense of duty to obey the official commands of his superior officer.

Your petitioners therefore humbly pray that Your Most Gracious Majesty may be pleased to take this matter into your most gracious consideration, and pardon and direct and order the release of the said George R. Witton, and your petitioners will in duty bound ever pray.

CHAPTER XXIV

THE LONG SUSPENSE

November and December passed over, and I was still confined to my bed. I had received a cable message from my brother that the Australian petition had closed with 100,000 signatures, and was now on its way to England; it was the largest petition that had ever left Australia. I now began to feel troubled that I would not be well enough to leave the prison when my release came. I was allowed to receive letters more frequently, as the rules are somewhat relaxed in regard to them when a prisoner is seriously ill.

When the medical officer visited me on Christmas Day he said I was now making good progress towards recovery, and if I kept on as I was going I would be able to get up the following week. "But," he added, "you will be convalescent for at least another three or four months, but that is nothing, you know, when one is in prison." "Four months!" I exclaimed "I hope to be home long before that." He seemed rather amused at my impetuosity, and said that he could not promise me.

The New Year was ushered in with the usual accompaniments of an English winter-fogs, drizzling rain, and bitter cold winds. Portland, too, is an exceedingly bleak spot, where cold winds and rain seem more prevalent than elsewhere.

On 3rd January I got up and dressed myself for the first time for nearly five months, but was too weak to walk a step. As soon as I had regained sufficient strength to move about, and there was no further fear of contagion, I was removed to another cell. During my illness and convalescence my door was never closed, a barred iron gate being used instead; this was a merciful concession which made my gloomy surroundings a little more cheerful, as I was able to see and hear a little of what was going on around me. I was visited by numerous Home Office officials, the Governor, and many others, also the medical director, with whom I had a long conversation about Australia and Australian industries, particularly the butter export industry and the use of boric acid as a preservative.

I was also on two occasions visited by Captain Harris, a prison inspector, a stout, thick-set man with a stern countenance and piercing grey eyes; he was known and feared by officers and prisoners alike. He had earned the reputation of being the strictest Governor the prison service had ever known; a prisoner could rely upon getting from him all he was entitled to, but a favour never.

During one of his rounds he visited the cell opposite mine, in which was located an elderly man who had once held a responsible position in civil life, but had fallen on evil days. Prison life had wrecked his nervous system, and was undermining his health. "Well, what is the matter with you?" said Captain Harris. "I--I--I--feel all broke up, sir," stammered the old fellow. "All broke up, broke up, how broke up, what do you mean?" said the inspector. "I'm all broke down, sir," was the abject reply of the prisoner. There was no mistaking it, either; every day was a torture to him. He eventually got his wish, and was transferred to Parkhurst.

One day the president of the Board of Visiting Magistrates came to see me; he told me he was in communication with the war Office, and wished to investigate my case, but I need not say anything to incriminate myself. I told him that I had no desire to conceal or disguise any of the facts or the events that had brought about my conviction; I had not acted with any criminal intent towards those against whom I was fighting, but had merely obeyed the orders of my superiors. I was daily expecting my release, and after this visit I became more impatient.

Up to this time the medical officer had not allowed my hair or beard to be cut, consequently I had five months' growth of hair on my head, and had also, cultivated an "Uncle Sam" beard. One day it was decided to have it trimmed with a pair of scissors, instead of the regulation prison clip; the warder and orderly came along with a comb and an antiquated pair of scissors, and set to work. The orderly cut and snipped until his arms ached; the warder then took the scissors and did likewise. The principal warder then came on the scene, took command of the situation and the tools, and finished the contract. This was, I believe, the most notable "hair-cut" in the history of the prison. After this ordeal I returned to my cell. Time passed slowly; every day was much alike in this land of gloom, I expected my release at any moment, and rapidly regained health and strength, and put on weight accordingly. When I was discharged from the infirmary I was heavier than I had ever been in my life before, turning the scales at a very little short of sixteen stone.

One afternoon the warder, with several "old lags" as assistants, was serving out the supper. One of the latter, a short, pugnacious-looking little character, stopped opposite my cell. I was standing at the gate, and I noticed this little fellow eyeing me very attentively from head to foot. When the warder's back was turned, he sidled up to me and suddenly whispered, "If I was as big as you I'd fight Sullivan" (referring to the champion American pugilist). And he looked as if he really meant it.

When I was strong enough to walk about, and weather permitted, I was allowed exercise in the fresh air for forty minutes every afternoon. What a treat those intervals were, and how I drank in the sharp, bracing air of the English springtime. For some time there was a lunatic in the cell next to mine; he walked behind me as we circled round at exercise. My nervous system had been greatly shaken, and it was not likely to be improved by having a madman walking close to my heels, who talked incessantly without sequence, and at times would break out into maniacal laughter. I usually got over the difficulty by falling out on some pretence or other-my shoestring required attention, perhaps. By some such little stratagem I would get him in front of me. I was not sorry when, after a determined attempt at suicide, he was transferred to Parkhurst.

After seven months in the infirmary my health was reestablished. As yet I had received no intimation as to the result of the petition; persistent efforts were still being made in Australia and South Africa to obtain my release. Further petitions had been sent from Australia, supported by members of the Federal and State Parliaments; resolutions had also been passed in my favour by both Houses of Parliament in Natal and Cape Colony; public meetings had been held throughout South Africa, and letters and circulars had been distributed throughout the Empire. Subscription lists had been opened to defray expenses, and a notable one was returned to the Treasurer by a ship's officer who had collected from the passengers. It included people from Nova Scotia, Ireland, Wales, Norway, England, Denmark, Scotland, Belgium, Russia, France, Germany, Palestine, and Japan. Innumerable petitions from public and private bodies and individuals were sent to the Home authorities asking for my release.

These were all referred to a War Office whose policy in Africa prevented them from dealing in such a quality as justice. This action of the War Office was greatly resented by the subjects of the Empire generally, and caused strong comment by the press in Australia, South Africa, and Canada.

About the middle of May I was discharged from the infirmary, and sent back to my 3 x 7 cubicle. I had heard that there were a few large cells in one of the wards, which had been formed by taking out a partition, thus making two cells into one. I interviewed the medical officer, and asked to be recommended for a larger cell. My request was granted; my quarters were then a little more habitable; the cell, being the second from the end of the hall, was better ventilated.

The next day I appeared on parade, to the great surprise of the majority of my fellow prisoners. Vague rumours had been in circulation; some had heard that I was dead, others that I had been released and had gone home. I returned to my old party and made another start at tinsmithing; here I became acquainted with the past life of some of my fellow-workmen. Most of them belonged to the genteel ranks of criminals. There were representatives of the medical fraternity, the Bar, the clergy, the stage, the army, and the navy; bank managers, company promoters, spiritualist mediums, and all sorts and conditions of men--all on an equality, all swelling the revenue of John Bull by making tin cans.

When I had been at this work about a month I found that the confinement of the workshop and the acid fumes were again impairing my health. I once more interviewed the medical officer. On this occasion I requested outdoor labour, and the following day I was transferred to 33 party, stone dressing. This party worked in the stone yards near the quarries, about three-quarters of a mile from the prison. I liked this work, and made very good progress. After I had been about a week at it I was complimented on the headway I had made in mastering the art of making "headers and stretchers." The work was in no way laborious, and there was the walk backwards and forwards twice a day; the opportunities of indulging in conversation were also more numerous.

While working in the stone shed I had for companions an M.D. on one side, and a well-known English champion prize-fighter on the other. One day I saw the champion of the art of self-defence, whom I will call C-03, give a little exhibition of his skill. There is a good deal of jealous spirit shown even in a prison; C-03 accused a fellow-prisoner of backbiting him, and watched for an opportunity to retaliate. The warder in charge just at the time had his head buried in the tool-chest, taking stock of the spare tools. C-03 made a dart like lightning, and with a blow nicely aimed at the jaw felled his maligner to the ground. I was the only person who saw it, and I went to the assistance of the fallen man, and tried to put him on his feet; he was limp and speechless. When the warder's attention had been attracted he inquired of me, "What is the matter with him?" "I think he has had a stroke, sir," I replied. The M.D. was called; he examined the man's pulse; he said it was throbbing and beating in a most erratic manner; the case puzzled him. However, a little cold water soon brought the man round. "What is the matter?" inquired the warder, "did you faint?" "I must have, though it is the first time I ever fainted in my life," was the reply. The sick man was eventually removed to the infirmary, where he was treated for some time for neuralgia.

There was also in the party a great burly Irishman, a very strong and powerful man, whose inclinations were strongly averse to any kind of labour. By some means he softened the heart of the medical officer, and was put on light labour, which consisted of breaking refuse stone into fine road metal; this was done in a sitting position. He had for a companion a little hunch-back cripple, whom out of fear he prevailed upon to collect and wheel to him all the stone to be broken. But when his burly companion monopolised all the smallest and soft pieces, and left the larger and hard chunks for his "little mate," it was time to protest. This the "little mate" did, and backed it up by dancing around the big man with a shovel, breathing out threatenings and slaughter. This necessitated the intervention of the warder, who read the "Riot Act" to both of them.

There was also another little old man, who had passed his three score years and ten, and was serving his first term of imprisonment. I saw him in the infirmary, when I was struck by the huge boots he wore, which he dragged along the ground as he walked. One day I got an opportunity to speak to him; I asked him why he did not change his boots for a better fit. The old fellow smiled, and replied that he got them like that on purpose, so as to be able to pull them on and off without unlacing them. His three years' term was nearing completion, so I asked him what he intended to do when he was released. "Have a glass and a pipe first," he readily replied. A glass of ale and a pipe of tobacco were evidently the greatest solace the future held for him. This case appealed to me very much; surely justice would not have been violated if his sentence had been suspended after a short part of it had been served.

Time went on; I worked and waited, and summer was now well advanced. I had fallen into the stereotyped routine of prison life, and had made up my mind to be civil and silent, and cause as little trouble as possible to those in authority over me. I could see that complaints or violence could accomplish nothing in one's favour in the long run; if the warders were interfered with they never lost a chance of getting their own back. A prisoner who does his work to the best of his ability and obeys all orders implicitly without comment, practically surrendering his individuality to the Governor and his satellites, and having no opinion of his own, is the best off.

I settled down to my work and did it tolerably well; I was often rewarded with a cheery word from the Governor or his deputy. One day in August the Deputy-Governor came to me while I was at work and said he was afraid he had bad news for me. The first thought that rushed through my mind was a family bereavement; it was my father, or perhaps my mother. He then added, "The petition for your release has been refused." I was staggered for a moment; this was indeed a heavy blow to me. I could not and would not believe that the King had declined to release me. I knew full well that the blocking of all progress to the efforts on my behalf was due to the obstinacy of the War Office; my hopes, however, were not altogether annihilated. I knew there was increased agitation throughout the Empire on my behalf, so I toiled on, and hoped and waited through the winter, which was a very severe one. Another Christmas and New Year's Day passed away, the third I had spent within prison walls.

Shortly after this the War Office was reorganised and the Army Council constituted. A slight turn in my favour then occurred, and in reply to a petition which I sent to the Home Secretary I was informed that the question of my release would be considered when I had completed a term of three years' imprisonment. This concession lifted a great weight from my mind. I did not let matters rest here; as soon as I had completed two years and three months, and had earned the number of marks representing a three years' sentence, I petitioned again for my release under the existing Classification and Remission System. Failing this, I asked that my term of imprisonment should date from the award of the sentence, instead of from the confirmation of the sentence, which occurred a month later. The latter request was granted, but I was informed that I must not expect my release until I had actually completed three years' imprisonment.

So to this fate I had for the time being to submit. I knew that at Capetown a meeting had been held and a powerful organisation formed, and strenuous efforts were being made for my immediate release. Messrs. W. B. Melville, Herbert Easton, and R. Bruce-Hardy, did Trojan work. An influential deputation waited on Sir Gordon Sprigg, the Cape Premier, with the object of enlisting his sympathy. The following is a summary of the proceedings, extracted from the South African press:--

A deputation of citizens waited upon the Premier, Sir Gordon Sprigg, with the object of enlisting his sympathy on behalf of the movement to secure the release of ex-Lieutenant Witton, of the Bushveldt Carbineers. Lieutenant Witton, it will be remembered, was tried with others by a court-martial in connection with certain military irregularities on the high veldt. He was sentenced to death, which sentence was commuted to imprisonment for life by Lord Kitchener. He is now a prisoner in an English gaol. The deputation consisted of the following gentlemen:--The Hon. J. H. Hofmeyr, and Messrs. J. W. Van Reenan, J. J. Michau, C. A. MacBride, R. Bruce-Hardy, B.A., W. B. Melville, C. R. Juchau, F. W. Wilson, G. W. Baudinet, Thomas Gibson, Drs. Forsyth and Crozier-Durham, Dr. Petersen, M.L.C., D. Van Zyl, ex-M.L.A., and Messrs. Herbert, Easton and D. McKey.

Mr. D. McKey, who introduced the deputation, said:-Sir, as a member of the recently-formed Constitutional Club of this city, which includes among its objects the maintenance of the glorious traditions of British justice and fair play, I have the honour to be one of the conveners of this deputation, which has been formed to ask you, as the Prime Minister of this colony, to use your influence in such a manner as you may deem best on behalf of our young fellowsubject, for some time known as Lieutenant Witton, but who is at present undergoing sentence for life in Portland Prison. When first approached upon this matter I was of opinion that it was a case which called for mercy alone, but upon hearing the statements of one of his fellow-officers, and that of others acquainted with the entire facts, I have come to the conclusion that there has been a grave miscarriage of justice in committing to prison for life one who I have every reason to believe is an innocent man, and, therefore, as it is justice alone that is sought, it is with that end in view that Mr. Easton and myself called upon and asked you to receive us here to-day, and I feel sure that our appeal for your assistance will not be made in vain. In forming this deputation we have endeavoured to make it non-political by inviting the leading representatives of both the Progressive and South African party, to each of whom we have written, giving at least seven, days' clear notice, and asking them to attend; and I therefore, hope, that whatever may be the outcome of our efforts on behalf of this unfortunate man, our motives will not be misconstrued, as our sole desire is to obtain his honourable release.

I have not considered it necessary to go fully into the details of the case, as there are others of this deputation who are in a position to, place the matter more fully before you. I will therefore ask Mr. Her-

167

bert Easton to address you, and I beg to thank you for the patient hearing which you have given me.

Mr. Herbert Easton said:--Sir Gordon,--Our object in meeting you to-day is to enlist your sympathy and secure your support towards a deep and far-spread movement to obtain the release of ex-Lieutenant Witton on the grounds of justice. We do not approach you to, ask mercy on his behalf, for, regarding him as innocent, we think it a scandal that this young officer is being detained in an English gaol.

The War Office is an administration that has lost the confidence of the people, and public feeling on the Witton case has been intensified by the tactics adopted by that discredited administrative board in resisting the, efforts of Witton's advocates to bring the true history of the case to light. The voluminous evidence taken at the courts-martial--on behalf of the War Office--remains withheld, and all official information so far published is that which has been subjected to the severest press censorship. Little by little the true history of Witton's connection with the B.V.C. has come out, and has made a profound impression on the popular mind, which is now filled with anxiety for what we believe to be the unjust fate of a British subject. (Hear, hear.) You, Sir Gordon, are fully aware of the extraordinary excitement caused by the Dreyfus case-how the military authorities of the great French Republic were so wilfully misled as to the accusation against Dreyfus; that it was only after the international-and particularly the British press roused such a great wave of feeling by minor discoveries, that the French Government suspected the verdict of the military court-martial, and was compelled to have Dreyfus retried before a civil tribunal, which fully justified the immense trouble and labour taken by the public in his cause. We here to-day feel convinced that we are voicing the sentiments of millions in saying that we believe a retrial of Witton before a civil tribunal will reveal a second Dreyfus case.

We are oppressed with the belief that the promises made to, the petitioners to have our statements and prayers brought directly under the notice of His Majesty the King have not in England been carried out to the spirit and the letter, as we, feel assured that, were it possible to reach the ear of His Majesty with the whole evidence, there would be no question that His Majesty would cause a retrial of Lieutenant Witton to be instituted.

In conclusion, Mr. Easton read the following letters Schoongezigt, Stellenbosch, 4th December, 1903.

Dear Sir,-I regret that a previous engagement to speak at the Paarl on the Chinese importation question will prevent me from joining your deputation. As a firm believer in the fullest possible measure of amnesty, I think that it would be good policy to release Witton. I do not wish to enter on the particulars of his crime, his trial, or his sentence, but upon the broad grounds of policy; I think that you have followed the right course in appealing to the Prime Minister of the colony to use his good offices in laying the case before the Imperial authorities, with whom the matter rests.

I am, dear Sir, yours faithfully, JOHN X. MERRIMAN.

De la Rey, Gardens, 5th December, 1903.

My dear Mr. Easton, I regret very much that I cannot form one of the deputation to interview the Prime Minister in connection with the Witton case. I have to leave on Monday early for Pietersburg to address the electors at several places in that district, where I am a candidate. I hope you will be successful. I cannot see any reason for believing that Sir Gordon Sprigg will not assist you in connection with your efforts re the Witton case.

Yours truly, C. Du P. CHIAPPINI.

"Ons Land," Kantoor, Kaapstad, 27th November, 1905.

Gentlemen,--I have the honour to acknowledge the receipt of your letter of even date with reference to "the Witton case," inviting, me to join a deputation which will wait upon the Prime Minister on Monday, 7th December, and I beg to state that I have the greatest sympathy with the object of the proposed deputation. I would consider it a privilege to be able to do something towards its attainment. I find, however, that it will be impossible for me to be present on that date, seeing that I have already arranged for a public meeting (announced in "Ons Land" of yesterday) at Vredenberg, Saldanha Bay, with my fellow-candidate, Mr. J. A. Smuts, for Saturday, 5th December, and that I shall not reach Capetown again before Tuesday evening, 8th December.

I sincerely regret that this previous engagement will prevent me from joining you in the deputation, but I wish you all success, and I shall do all in my power to assist you.

Believe me, gentlemen, to be, yours faithfully, F. S. MALAN.

Mr. W. B. Melville, who was deputed to state the case for Witton, said:--

"We are grateful, Sir Gordon, for the opportunity you are affording us to-day to lay before you, as the head of His Majesty's Government in this free country, the case of Lieutenant Witton. Your readiness to receive us, and to listen to what we have to say is courtesy and consideration characteristic of you, and appreciated by us. It will be our aim to represent to you to the best of our ability the broad circumstances and salient features of the case as they bear on the innocence of Witton of any act of barbarism or criminal complicity in connection with the tragedies on the high veldt in August, 1901. At the outset, we desire to dissociate ourselves from any defence of the murders and other brutalities which blacken the record of some members of the Bushveldt Carbineers; but we do say that it is unfair to assume that any more than a small percentage of that irregular corps is directly, or indirectly, responsible for crimes that cried to heaven for vengeance. Unfortunately retributive justice, in blind pursuit of the guilty, punished, in at least one instance, the innocent. You will gather from this that we regard the court-martial proceedings as incomplete, and seriously unsatisfactory. As the responsibility of Witton's sad position rests with the court-martial, and as the strength of our position is the imperfect character of that tribunal, perhaps it would be well to state at once how it was possible for that court to fail in arriving at the truth. In the first place it was hurriedly summoned, and sat for three weeks dealing with a host of charges against the Bushveldt Carbineers. Counsel for the defence (Major Thomas) appeared in court forthwith, as he had no time for the preparation of the many cases entrusted to him. He had scarcely a statement to guide him, and was only confronted with evidence while the trials proceeded. There was no chance of testing credibility, and there was little opportunity of sifting evidence. Evidence objected to was admitted, and rebutting evidence, available under ordinary circumstances, was unobtainable. The defence, not designedly, but none the less regrettably, was hampered throughout. The period was scarcely favourable to calm judicial temperament, and the accused were prejudiced by the stories current regarding the barbarities of the Bushveldt Carbineers. These barbarities were bad enough, but report made them infinitely worse. The men on trial had to bear the full brunt of every crime, real or imaginary, attributed to the corps. Witton, being one of the accused, had his case prejudiced with the rest. The headquarters of the military were impressed with the necessity of decisive action to counteract the effects of the international wave of horror created by the reports from the high veldt. Necessarily, the mind of the court-martial--in direct touch with Army Headquarters-was imbued with little official sympathy with the men on trial. We do not infer that the court-martial was corrupt; we do say it had been unconsciously influenced by its environment. If the same court-martial sat to-day, its proceedings would be widely different, and its conclusions more in conformity to British justice. We trust, therefore, Sir Gordon, that you will bear in mind the all too rough and ready character of the court-martial. However much it sufficed for the period at Pietersburg, its deliberations and decisions must not be held, at this later and quieter date, to be beyond review and reversal when a precious human life is fretting within the walls of an English prison.

"We understand that you, Sir Gordon, have devoted some attention to this case, and that the evidence published in the London 'Times' of 18th April, 1902, may have come before you. That evidence does not fill a page in the 'Times,' whereas the court-martial proceedings extended to three weeks. Not more than one-twentieth part of the evidence has been made public. Press censorship was responsible for the elimination of questions and answers not deemed judicious for public examination during the war. Since the signing of peace the War Office has not been called upon to produce for public inspection the whole of the evidence. It is most unfortunate that the papers--the missing papers--have been so completely hidden from view. We now ask your assistance in procuring a certified copy of the whole of the evidence, believing that such will be sufficient to establish innocence, in Witton's case at least.

"As to the condensed and sharply-censored report of the evidence, we desire to say little. As it has been tampered with, it is almost valueless. Nevertheless, it does not disclose the guilt of Witton, even though it infers it. But it does not assist the inquiry. It merely mystifies it."

The connecting links in the Witton story have been gathered from many sources, chiefly from those who gave evidence, or who were present to give evidence, and were not called, or who were not asked to be present at the court-martial. It is necessary to narrate everything about which there is general agreement.

Here is a copy of a letter addressed by the Church of England chaplain to Handcock's widow. It will explain much that is dark and mysterious in the Witton case:--

"Dear Madam,--I was military chaplain at Pietersburg, in the Northern Transvaal, during all the time that the Bushveldt Carbincers had their headquarters there, and I knew your late husband and all those officers and men who were concerned, for and against, in his trial, and I attended most of the sittings of the courts. And, knowing what I know, I want to say to you that, great as may be your grief for the loss of him, you need feel no shame, but rather pride, on his account. He was a good-hearted man, and a brave soldier, simple and fearless, and he did what he was told. If he did wrong-I do not say that he did-it was the fault of his superiors, who gave him their orders. In the matter of the shooting of the Boer prisoners, of which he and others were found guilty, he acted under the orders of Lieutenant Morant, a man of strong feelings and eager to avenge the savage murder of his friend Captain Hunt.

"In the matter of the shooting of the missionary, the only one of the crimes charged which really excited any moral indignation, the court, without hesitation, found him not guilty, and never, I should think, has a feebler charge been brought before a court.

"I was not a friend of these officers of the Bushveldt Carbineers, but my sympathy was aroused by the harsh treatment they received-in being kept in close arrest (I myself, the chaplain, was requested not to visit them) for some months before they were tried, and by the way the case was, as it were, prejudged from the statements of bad men, and by the utterly false accounts which were inserted in English and, I believe, Australian papers.

"I did not see your husband after he was taken down to Pretoria, but I understand that he died simply and fearlessly, as he had lived.

"I have heard it said that the execution convinced the Boers of British fairness, and made them ready to come to terms. If this be so, then Lieutenants Morant and Handcock died for their country in a very special sense, and this is one of the many instances of suffering, even if undeserved, bringing salvation."

"With much sympathy and good wishes, I am yours very truly, JOSHUA BROUGH."

Now, as to Lieutenant Robertson, who gave evidence against his brother officers. During the long imprisonment of the men before they were shot, and the others who escaped the death penalty, he was retained in Pretoria as a witness, and allowed #1 a day expenses. He had afterwards a first-class passage to England and back.

As to the witnesses for the prosecution, whose statements were more or less conflicting, some of them boasted openly that they expected to be rewarded with farms. This will show how much their evidence merited reliance. I had an opportunity while in Pretoria, in June of last year, of discussing the case with many ex-irregulars of the Bushveldt Carbineers. Those who had volunteered evidence against their officers would scarcely favourably impress a jury of citizens. Decent young fellows complained that they had not been called for the defence. The conviction of Witton, they declared, fairly staggered them. They begged of me, with no simulated emotion, to do my utmost as a journalist to bring out the truth and to rescue as speedily as possible Witton from the dungeon he did not deserve, for his humanity was apparent throughout his military career, when a ruder nature would have been absolutely corrupted. I promised these young men to do my utmost, and, although effort after effort has resulted in failure, we do not despair of abstracting Witton's case from its musty pigeon-hole in the War Office. I leave to other members of the deputation a statement of what we have done on Witton's behalf.

The War Office assures us that "there are no extenuating circumstances in Witton's case." The French Minister for War assured the Republic-and the world-that there was no doubt about the guilt of Dreyfus. The Empire's Dreyfus case is the Witton scandal. It is a greater peril to Empire than a conspiracy of the Powers. Let justice be done and honour vindicated, even though the delicate susceptibilities of the War Office be perturbed thereby.

Mr. Bruce-Hardy spoke on the legal aspect of the case as follows:--Sir Gordon Sprigg,-I am afraid that after the eloquent speech of my worthy friend Mr. Melville, I can say but little that will be of any great assistance to this deputation. One point, however, I might put some slight stress on, and that is the legal aspect of the case. Firstly, I would like to cite a clause out of the Army Regulations and Manual of Military Law of 1899, viz., part 1, sec. 9:--"Every person subject to military law who commits the following offence, that is to say, disobeys in such manner as to show a wilful defiance of authority any lawful command given personally by his superior officer in the execution of his office, whether the same is given orally or in writing, or by signal or otherwise, shall, on conviction by court-martial, be liable to suffer death or such less punishment as in this Act mentioned." Now I think the above Act is very plain, and I would take it that in this case it implies that had he (ex-Lieutenant Witton) disobeyed the order given him by his superior officer to shoot the now deceased, he (Witton) would have been guilty of a misdemeanour, and would have been liable to be shot. But to come to the point, we ascertained that ex-Lieutenant Witton did at the time oppose the shooting of the deceased. He stated that as a junior officer he would have to carry out the order of his superior, but he did so under protest; therefore again I might say that I fail to see how this ex-Lieutenant has committed any crime. The only point, as far as I can ascertain, that could be brought up against him is that, having received instructions from his senior in command, he protested, which would be but a slight misdemeanour or offence. But he has not been tried on that account. He was tried for murder, and has been sentenced to penal servitude for life. I must confess that I fail to see where this man has obtained justice. Undoubtedly, if he had disobeyed his orders, he would probably have been sentenced to death or imprisonment. It appears clear that had ex-Lieutenant Witton obeyed or disobeyed he would have been found guilty. Therefore I would submit that this man is, according to Army Regulations, innocent, and I trust that you, Sir Gordon, will see this matter in its true light, and use your best endeavours and advocate a reopening of this case before a civil tribunal.

Mr. C. R. Juchau, who spoke next, referred to what had already been done in this matter locally. Continuing, he said:--Shortly before the arrival in Cape Colony of the ex-Colonial Secretary, a meeting was held, at which it was decided to prepare a petition for signatures, and a deputation was appointed to wait on the right hon. gentleman with the petition, and ask him to lay the matter before His Majesty the King. Mr. Chamberlain would not receive the deputation, but would take the petition and place it before the King. This promise we agreed on was not fulfilled. Meetings were held also in Johannesburg and Pretoria, the Boer Generals giving their hearty support to the movement; and this we submit, argues well for the justice of our cause. Sir Arthur Lawley, however, has stated that in Witton's case there were no extenuating circumstances. This, we hold, is a very unfair and most infamous decision in the face of the facts. As you are aware, sir, all our efforts so far have been fruitless, but we are determined to persevere. The press throughout the world has recently been written to and asked to lend its powerful influence to get the case reopened and the full evidence published. Our labours are purely humanitarian, and we are determined to see justice done the unfortunate ex-officer. With regard to one point dealt with in re the shooting of Boer prisoners for wearing khaki, I do not think the authorities concerned will deny the following case which came under my notice. Colonel Cookson's column operated in the Western Transvaal during the later stages of the war. About April, 1902, two Boers were caught in Reitvlei district, about 40 miles from Klerksdorp, and one of these men was drumheaded and shot for wearing a British khaki uniform-I believe by a firing party from B squadron (Major Scott) Damant's Horse. As a trooper of Cookson's column, I know that none of the officers concerned were court-martialled up to the declaration of peace.

Captain Baudinet cited the case of the shooting of Baxter, a Boer, for wearing khaki by the order of Colonel Scobell, and up to the time of the signing of peace he had not heard that Colonel Scobell had been tried by court-martial. He had offered at the time of Witton's trial to give evidence on Witton's behalf, but was assured any exculpatory evidence would be superfluous.

Mr. J. W. Van Reenan, an ex-officer of high rank in the army of the late Free State, said that on the subject of khaki he wished to make some pointed remarks, inasmuch as previous to the outbreak of hostilities khaki clothing was ordered to be, purchased for the use of the Boer forces. In support of that statement he added that he had to produce vouchers from the various merchants who supplied the cloth. British prisoners captured by the burgher forces on many occasions informed him that orders had been given by British officers that all Boer prisoners found wearing khaki were liable to be shot. Consequently, under these circumstances, he could quite understand the difficulty and uncertainty which must have arisen in the minds of junior officers in carrying out such instructions from superiors.

Sir Gordon Sprigg said he had listened with great interest to the speeches of the deputation, and was impressed with the very remarkable features of the case. In many respects they were unique, and he could quite understand that there was widespread public interest taken in the case. He would at once say that he was in sympathy with the wishes of those who desired to see the early release of the young Victorian officer. He could quite understand the difficulties of a court-martial sitting during military operations arriving at just decisions. He would go into the case very carefully, and could promise them that he would put the appeal in the proper quarters in the strongest terms.

CHAPTER XXV

FREEDOM AT LAST!

A reply was received some time later by Mr. Easton from the Premier's secretary, stating that the Premier had received a despatch from the Colonial Secretary, who said that the Secretary of State for War was of opinion that the time had not yet arrived for advising His Majesty to grant my pardon.

Affidavits were secured from E. Hammett, late Sergeant-Major in the Bushveldt Carbineers, and R. Maynard, also a late member of that ill-fated corps; they were as follows:--

I, Ernest Hammett, Squadron Sergeant-Major, late Bushveldt Carbineers, of Taunton, in the County of Somerset, make oath and say as follows:--

1. That on 20th June, 1901, I joined the Bushveldt Carbineers at Capetown. On the 24th June, 1901, I proceeded to join my regiment, then stationed at Pietersburg, Transvaal.

2. That on 2nd August, 1901, I received orders to join the detachment at the Spelonken, some seventy miles north of Pietersburg, which was commanded by Lieutenant Morant. Lieutenant Witton was the officer in charge of the convoy, which left Pietersburg on 3rd August, 1901, and I, being the senior noncommissioned officer, had many opportunities of conversing with him, and found him to be a thorough

officer and a gentleman. We arrived at Spelonken on the 4th August, 1901, at 5 p.m.

3. I am positive that in all the operations in which Lieutenant Witton and myself were engaged, Lieutenant Witton carried out to the strict letter of the law the orders he received from his superior officer only. And therefore I fail to see how he could be held responsible for any regrettable orders given by Lieutenant Morant.

4. Lieutenant Morant and Lieutenant Handcock, who were shot at the old Pretoria gaol on 27th February, 1902, were senior officers to Lieutenant Witton, all being Australians, and, I may add, not drilled to the discipline that is traditional to the ordinary British officers; but for hard work and fighting propensities I never fell in with three braver or more humane gentlemen during my fifteen years' military career.

5. I was arrested on the 24th October, 1901, with the officers of the Bushveldt Carbineers, and detained in the Pietersburg prison until 1st January, 1902, when I was, for some reason never made known to me, released with Lieutenant Hannam.

I, Robert Maynard, make oath and say:--

1. I was a member of the Bushveldt Carbineers on active service in the high veldt, North Transvaal, and took part in the operations against the Boers.

2. I was acquainted with Lieutenant Witton, and verily believe that Lieutenant Witton at all times carried out to the strict letter of the law the orders he received from his superior officers.

3. In those particular incidents which led to his becoming court-martialled and convicted he was merely carrying out the orders received from his superior officers.

Many paragraphs, verses, comments, and illustrations on my case appeared from time to time in the press in different parts of the world.

FREEDOM AT LAST!

This is from "The Owl," South Africa:

Now list to the tale of an injured man-- As ever a one was he-- Who is eating his heart in durance vile, While those who should suffer can laugh and smile, And pick their own company.

He came from the land of the kangaroo-- From a land of men, I trow-- To fight or die for Old England's right, To risk the peril, obey the might That should order him to or fro.

But an order came, in the course of time, Hard for a man to do; For life, after all, is a precious thing, And it isn't so easy to sever the string When it comes to me or you.

But you must not falter, or reason why, In the deadly time of war. You must simply do as you're told to do By those in authority over you, Or what is authority for?

He obeyed, as a son of the Empire should, Nor stopped to count the cost; The result was the same, with authority's name, As though he had done it for personal fame, His case was entirely lost.

And so, to abide with the vile and corrupt They sent him to prison away, To languish and pine for his freedom divine; Though they made it for life, yet I think there's a sign That he has not much longer to stay.

Just about this time Major Lenehan had been reinstated in the Commonwealth forces. To use his own words, he had a terrible battle the lying reports that had been published had discredited the Carbineers in the eyes of the public. Ultimately he succeeded in obtaining the sympathy of one Australian Government, with the above result.

In June, 1904, I received a message informing me that my father was seriously ill, and that Mr. Hughes, the then Minister for External affairs, had been interviewed, and it had been suggested to him that, as the Imperial authorities had agreed to consider the, question of my release in the following February, they might be again approached. Mr. Hughes brought the request before the Prime Minister, and a cable message was sent, rehearsing the facts with respect to, my dying father, and intimating that it would be regarded as a gracious act if my immediate release were granted.

To this the Hon. A. G. Lyttelton, Secretary of State for the Colonies, replied on 21st June, the date of my father's death, that he was not disposed to depart from the promise made by the military authorities to reconsider my sentence in February, 1905. Early in July, being still ignorant of my father's death, I again petitioned, asking for my release on account of his serious illness; to this petition I did not receive any reply.

Just at this time the Hon. J. D. Logan, M.L.C., of Capetown, arrived in England. He was a doughty champion of my cause, and enlisted the sympathy of many of the members of the House of Commons on my behalf, particularly that of Major Eustace Jamieson, M.P., who, after much battling and buffeting, induced the authorities to grant my release. Not expecting this to be accomplished for several days, Mr. Logan returned to his home in Scotland. Upon arrival at Cardross House, in Perthshire, he found a telegram waiting for him to the effect that the prisoner Witton would be handed over to him at once. This meant returning immediately to England. Mr. Logan was completely knocked up, and hardly felt equal to the task, but he ordered out his motor car, caught the midnight express at Stirling, and arrived in London the following morning.

My case had been brought forward in the House of Commons during the night of 10th August. Mr. Churchill asked the Secretary of State for War whether he could now state the intention of His Majesty's Government in respect to Witton; to this question Mr. Arnold-Foster replied, "His Majesty the King has been pleased to order that Witton be released." (Cheers.)

The first intimation I received that my sentence had been remitted, and that I was at last free, was imparted to me by the Governor of the prison in his private office, on Thursday, 11th August. He asked me if I knew the Hon. J. D. Logan or Major Jamieson. I replied that I was not personally acquainted with either of those gentlemen.

"Well," he said, "I have just received a telegram instructing me to hand you over to them; they will be here at three o'clock to take you away. There is not much time to get you fitted out; however, we will do the best we can for you." After being handed several congratulatory telegrams I was hurried away to the separate cells.

Here I began to collect my thoughts. So at last the glad tidings had come, and in two hours I would pass the barrier that separated the bond from the free. My joy was unutterable, yet it was tinged with one regret-I wished that it had come a little sooner. I had received the news that my father had passed away, and I felt that the knowledge that I had gained my freedom would have gladdened his heart in his last hours.

At the cells I was waited upon by the tailor and shoemaker, who took a rough measurement for clothes and boots; after this a hurried visit was paid to the photographer's studio. Here I took off my prison jacket and donned a coat of mufti, many sizes too small for me, and a collar that fastened at the back; an antiquated, faded tie completed the civilian outfit. In a few minutes two photographs were taken, also finger prints on the Bertillon system of identification.

Upon returning to my cell the master tailor brought me an outfit of clothes, the, largest size in stock. I cast off my prison garb and donned a suit of dark green tweed, a suit which proclaims every wearer to the world as an ex-convict. When I dressed myself the trousers required to be turned up at the bottom, and the sleeves at the wrists, but I was satisfied. I did not ask for anything different. The tailor inspected me and remarked, "It's not a bad fit after all."

I was then taken again to the office of the Governor. By this time Mr. Logan and Mr. Herbert Kitson, his private secretary, had arrived. On being ushered in, Mr. Logan came forward and congratulated me on regaining my freedom, and informed me that he intended taking me to Scotland for some grouse shooting. The Governor then handed me over some money that had been lodged with him by my brother pending my release, also a sum of thirty shillings earned by industry and good conduct during my incarceration. I was not furnished with any formal discharge from His Majesty's prison until some weeks later. I was handed over to Mr. Logan, and after being warmly congratulated by the Governor and his deputy, we passed out through the barrier; then the gates rolled back, and I entered again into my freedom. More than one officer came up and wrung my hand, and wished me good luck.

A carriage was in waiting outside, and we hurriedly drove to the railway station. My first thoughts were to send the good news to my relatives in Australia, and from Weymouth a cablegram was despatched to my brother. This was hardly necessary, as the news had flashed round the world before it had been imparted to me. We reached Waterloo station at 9 o'clock, and drove to the Hotel Metropole for dinner. Here I met Major Jamieson, M.P., and expressed to him my warmest thanks for his efforts on my behalf. As we sat down to dinner I could not help thinking of the dinner I had with the late officers of the Carbineers the night before we left Pietersburg, when we were in happy expectation of freedom the following morning.

After a few hours' rest we drove to Euston, and boarded the midnight express for the North. I tried to sleep but could not; so much had been crowded into the last few hours that my brain seemed in a whirl. At eight in the morning we arrived at Stirling, where Mr. Logan's chaffeur was waiting at the station with the car. In half an hour we arrived at Cardross House, Mr. Logan's shooting-box in Perthshire. As soon as breakfast was over the guns were brought out, and we joined the other guests, who had made an early start on Flanders Moss; just eighteen hours after leaving Portland I shot my first grouse. The ladies joined us for lunch, making a pleasure party of twelve. This, my first luncheon on the moors, was to me a notable one; speeches and toasts were indulged in, and here I made my first speech.

My host, the Hon. James D. Logan, member of the Cape Legislative Council, is a popular figure in South African circles, where he is universally known as the "Laird of Matjesfontein." This genial son of Scotia was born at Reston, Berwickshire. He is the life and soul of South African sport, and at one time took a South African cricket eleven to England at his own expense. When the war began he raised a corps at Matjesfontein, and did excellent service at the front; he had his horse shot under him at Belmont.

Those weeks I spent with Mr. Logan I look back upon as the brightest in my life, being such a contrast to the abode of gloom I had so suddenly left.

FREEDOM AT LAST!

On 29th September I embarked at Liverpool on the White Star liner "Runic" for Australia; the passenger list totalled 500. Splendid weather was experienced during our run to Capetown.

At Capetown the "Runic" remained in port only a few hours. Here I was met and warmly welcomed back to South Africa by Mr. and Mrs. Herbert Easton, Mr. Bruce Hardy, Mr. Palmer, and other members of the Capetown Release Committee, who had done such excellent work in making the facts of my case so universally known.

On the 12th November 1904, after a chequered experience extending over nearly five years, I placed my foot again on my native soil. On my arrival in Australia I met among others Mr. Wainwright, general secretary of the Australian Natives' Association, and his son, Mr. Austin Wainwright, who so ably assisted my brother in his efforts towards my release. I also met Mr. Alfred Deakin, a true compatriot, who during his term of office as Prime Minister of the Commonwealth had been untiring in his efforts to secure my liberty and return to Australia.

You may also enjoy ...

Wandering Between Two Worlds: Essays on Faith and Art
Anita Mathias
Benediction Books, 2007
152 pages
ISBN: 0955373700

Available from www.amazon.com, www.amazon.co.uk
www.wanderingbetweentwoworlds.com

In these wide-ranging lyrical essays, Anita Mathias writes, in lush, lovely prose, of her naughty Catholic childhood in Jamshedpur, India; her large, eccentric family in Mangalore, a sea-coast town converted by the Portuguese in the sixteenth century; her rebellion and atheism as a teenager in her Himalayan boarding school, run by German missionary nuns, St. Mary's Convent, Nainital; and her abrupt religious conversion after which she entered Mother Teresa's convent in Calcutta as a novice. Later rich, elegant essays explore the dualities of her life as a writer, mother, and Christian in the United States-- Domesticity and Art, Writing and Prayer, and the experience of being "an alien and stranger" as an immigrant in America, sensing the need for roots.

About the Author

Anita Mathias was born in India, has a B.A. and M.A. in English from Somerville College, Oxford University and an M.A. in Creative Writing from the Ohio State University. Her essays have been published in The Washington Post, The London Magazine, The Virginia Quarterly Review, Commonweal, Notre Dame Magazine, America, The Christian Century, Religion Online, The Southwest Review, Contemporary Literary Criticism, New Letters, The Journal, and two of HarperSanFrancisco's The Best Spiritual Writing anthologies. Her non-fiction has won fellowships from The National Endowment for the Arts; The Minnesota State Arts Board; The Jerome Foundation, The Vermont Studio Center; The Virginia Centre for the Creative Arts, and the First Prize for the Best General Interest Article from the Catholic Press Association of the United States and Canada. Anita has taught Creative Writing at the College of William and Mary, and now lives and writes in Oxford, England.

CPSIA information can be obtained
at www.ICGtesting.com
Printed in the USA
BVHW071557250819
556721BV00002B/191/P